ABBEY NATIONAL
CONVERSION TO PLC

BY MARGARET REID

The Inside Story of Abbey National's
Conversion and Flotation

A Pencorp Book
in the Pencorp Management Series

Published by:
Pencorp Books
Beagle House
80 Hill Top
London NW11 6EE
Tel: 081-458 9343
Fax 081-455 7828

Copyright © Margaret Reid

ISBN: 1 870092 03 1

All rights reserved. No part of this book may be reproduced in any form or by any electronic or mechanical means, including information storage and retrieval systems, without permission in writing from the publisher, except by a reviewer who may quote brief passages in a review.

Set in 9 pt Bookman and printed by Biddles Ltd., Waltree House, Woodbridge Park, Guildford, Surrey GU1 1DA.

Designed by   The Production House London.

CONTENTS

		Page
Acknowledgements		i
Preface		v
Chapter One	A Breakfast Launch	1
Chapter Two	The Old Order Changes	11
Chapter Three	A New Law and a New Boss	25
Chapter Four	To Be, Or Not To Be, a PLC	37
Chapter Five	Cliveden Climax	47
Chapter Six	Designing the Scheme	61
Chapter Seven	A Court Cliffhanger	69
Chapter Eight	Planning in Millions	81
Chapter Nine	Enter AMAF	95
Chapter Ten	On The Road	105
Chapter Eleven	A Licence to Bank	113
Chapter Twelve	Voted Through	125
Chapter Thirteen	"Well, er .... Yes"	137
Chapter Fourteen	The Float and The Quote	147
Chapter Fifteen	The Thunderclap	163
Chapter Sixteen	Retrospect and Prospect	177
Index		

ACKNOWLEDGEMENTS

IT WAS a great pleasure to be asked to write the story of such a major event in the financial world as Abbey National's conversion and flotation. My satisfaction was the greater because the commission arose in November 1989, a time not long after the lengthily-prepared change of status had been accomplished. This meant that the memories of the many who had taken part in this unique corporate enterprise were still fresh as to the innumerable details, as well as the complex principal aspects, of the operation.

At times it seemed that the dozens of interviews undertaken and the information available to me were so full and interesting that my task, in the limited allotted timespan, had taken on something of the arduous nature which, for many of the participants involved in this momentus event, characterised the conversion operation itself.

That I have been able to complete this fascinating undertaking is due to the generous help of many people both at Abbey National and elsewhere and to them all I wish to express my thanks.

The board of Abbey National have freely allowed me to examine all the records I needed in connection with my research. They have also carefully respected my independence.

In addition, Sir Campbell Adamson and a number of his board and management colleagues spared time for lengthy and unhurried interviews in which they answered all my questions. These included Peter Davis, Jeremy Rowe, Sir John Garlick, Dame Jennifer Jenkins, Sara Morrison, Peter Birch, John Bayliss, John Fry, James Tyrrell, Charles Villiers, and John Ellis.

Ian Treacy was invaluable in helping me find the many documents I needed to study as well as acting as my link to his colleagues.

Elsewhere within Abbey National, Jane Ageros, Stewart Gowans, Phil Hallatt, Ian Harley, Ian Hart, Malcolm Holdsworth, Graeme Johnston and Brian Leary were unstinting. I was helped in addition by the written recollections of a number of members of Abbey's staff and others whom I did not meet personally.

Abbey National's advisers have also been generous with their time and in their readiness to discuss with me the subject of my study.

Especially helpful in guiding me through the legal and other intricacies have been Nicholas Wilson and Tim Clark of Slaughter & May, Abbey's City legal advisers, David Clementi, John Williams and Tim Wise of Kleinwort Benson, Abbey's merchant banking advisers, Jim Hamilton of Kleinwort Benson Securities, Abbey's joint brokers, Peter Jeffrey and Ian Brooks of Coopers & Lybrand Deloitte, Abbey's auditors and accountant advisers, Stuart Stradling and David Freud, both of Warburg Securities, and John Harben of Broad Street Associates.

The Rt. Hon. Ian Stewart, MP, formerly economic secretary to The Treasury, provided the important political perspective. My gratitude is similarly due to Michael Bridgeman and Terry Mathews of the Building Societies Commission, to Brian Gent at the Bank of England and to Martin Hall, formerly of The Treasury.

Mark Boleat of the Building Societies Association and of the Council of Mortgage Lenders was most generous in pointing me towards many important sources of information concerning the building societies.

I should also like to record my gratitude for the explanation and information about Abbey Members Against Flotation (AMAF) given to me by the late Alexander Sandison.

More personally, I want to express my thanks to my brother, Sir Martin Reid, not only for supporting me with constant encouragement throughout my task, but for making some valuable points about my treatment of the subject.

I also want to record my warm thanks for the great help generously provided to me by Lorna Kingdon who gave me an extra pair of hands to transfer this work into the word prcessor.

Finally I would like to add my thanks to Arnold Kransdorff, my editor and publisher, for his support and good-humoured encouragement.

London
March 1991.

PREFACE

ABBEY NATIONAL, as Britain's second largest building society and one of its best-known financial names, has long been known as a pioneer of developments in the money world. The lead it took in 1983 over the break-up of the societies' interest rate cartel was just one among many examples down the years of its instinct for innovation.

Thus it was no surprise that Abbey should have been the society which, in the late-1980s, seized the new opportunity to transform itself from a customer-owned "mutual" entity into a commercial banking company.

The elaborate operation to bring about this change and the simultaneous flotation on the Stock Exchange - successful, though far from without incident - was notable in many ways.

It strikingly reflected the deregulatory spirit of the times. It had many unique features and complexities as a ground-breaking corporate undertaking. And it is now serving as a catalyst of fresh changes in the financial world.

Nothing like a building society's conversion from its time-honoured mutual status would have been thinkable in Britain before the late-1970s. Up to that point, different sectors of financial activity such as banking, building society business, stockbroking, insurance, and more, kept within their own bounds, and links among them were few. Forms of organisation varied, building societies all being mutual, most banks being shareholder-owned companies and the insurance industry being a mixture of company and mutuals.

As to geographical spread, building societies were essentially domestic operations while banks, though chiefly UK-oriented, had gone some way in branching out abroad. General insurance companies were often international in character while stockbrokers were exclusively UK-owned with only small overseas interests.

Moreover, these patterns of operation and ownership were slow in changing, if they did so at all. Only occasionally, for instance, did mutual life insurance groups become shareholder companies.

Legal frameworks, regulatory systems and more impalpable conventions kept different sectors in their separate operating areas.

Building societies, for example, were confined by law to a narrow range of business, essentially the provision of first mortgage home-loans and the raising of retail savings to finance these - and closely associated - activities. The regulating legislation did not provide for the societies to be in anything but mutual form.

All this began to change, however, with the competition-fostering, "de-regulating" approaches of the Thatcher government in Britain and the Reagan administration in the United States from the start of the 1980s. Also increasing the pressures towards barrier reduction was the growing technology-led internationalisation of financial business, the result of electronic gadgetry's putting London, New York, Tokyo and other points round the globe in instant touch.

With these trends spurring financial groups to venture more widely in quest of business, old sector and geographical divides started to crumble, facilitating new initiatives and the formation of new groupings. In the US, the scrapping of old interest rate curbs triggered much innovation, competition and diversification.

In Britain, the abolition of the Stock Exchange commission cartel and the old broker-jobber split paved the way for the 1986 "Big Bang" and the buying up of the bulk of the former independent partnerships by large banks. Moves towards a post-1992 single market in the European Community have also stimulated inter-sector link-ups and ties across frontiers for the sake of competitive strength.

It was against this fast-changing background that the building societies sought and gained a broader operating framework in the Building Societies Act 1986, which also introduced the "PLC option" which Abbey National subsequently embraced.

This deregulatory context, in which Abbey National chose to seek its members' consent for an innovatory switch to company and bank status, makes its move a landmark in business history. The prolonged process by which this large financial institution worked out its policy and then became the first society to test the Act's newly-created conversion procedures adds further to the interest.

The sheer magnitude of the processes of having repeatedly to communicate with five million members make Abbey National's conversion and flotation a unique enterprise, as did much else about it. As one Abbey staff member much involved remarked: "Everything was a superlative."

The lengthy and careful decision-making and planning, the legal complications, the extensive financial and Stock Exchange preparations involving raising a huge £975 million and the vast scale of the logistics has made the operation a unique experience for everyone involved.

For the writer fortunate enough to have access to the material and opinions behind the headlines, and to be able to write of these events in their political and financial setting, it is a story that has almost everything; the novelty, the uniqueness, the difficulties, the scale - including the largest shareholder list of any UK company - and the personalities make the subject a fascinating one.

So does the inside story of the one serious mishap which marred the process - the destruction of hundreds of thousands of share certificates which necessitated rapid action to restore the situation.

Whether Abbey's change of status will be a trend-setter still remains to be seen since no other society has yet followed its rival's difficult road. But already its changeover has provoked rethinking on the status and powers of societies generally, with demands for the Act's updating.

As to Abbey National itself, while the full effects of its change of status have yet to unfold, this major quoted High Street banking group, with its chosen specialistion in personal financial services, will assuredly keep everyone guessing.

1

A BREAKFAST LAUNCH

WEDNESDAY, July 12, 1989, which dawned with all the brilliance of that remarkable summer, was a special day for the City of London and for Abbey National, Britain's second largest building society. For on that day Abbey National was shedding the long-standing mutual status it had had from its 19th Century self-help beginnings. From being a body unrelated to outside interests and deemed to be owned by its members - the savers and borrowers - it was joining the corporate sector.

Through this "conversion" it was becoming the first society to change into a public limited company - a so-called PLC - ranking as a bank in the same league as the big High Street groups. The transformation was being carried out through a scheme bringing a free hand-round of one hundred shares to the five million Abbey savers and home-buyers, making them the PLC's first shareholders.

At the same time, the new Abbey National PLC - the word "Bank" being left out to preserve the friendly image - was being floated on the Stock Exchange, where its shares were destined to be among the most actively traded of any stocks. As a preliminary, and in order to launch itself in full strength, it was raising, entirely from among its newly-created shareholders, nearly £975 million of fresh capital against extra shares.

The vast planning and paperwork involved in this two-part conversion/flotation operation made it, in the words of John Fry, the Abbey director who piloted the whole process, "on the scale of two giant privatisations." At a stroke the whole operation would bestow shares on millions of people who had never before held Stock Exchange investments, so giving Britain's share-owning population its biggest-ever boost to more than 12 million.

To complete the complex formalities before the first price "quote" could tick over brokers' screens, a top-level gathering was assembled that July morning at the City headquarters of Kleinwort Benson, Abbey's merchant bank.

Sir Campbell Adamson, the cordial 67-year-old industrialist who had been Abbey's chairman since 1978 and done much to guide the project, was there to play his part in its climax. So too was Peter Birch, 51, the cool, firm-handed chief executive from a former commercial background to whose will and resolve many would allot a key role in the lengthily-discussed decision to convert.

Prominent also was John Fry, a director and the PLC planner-in-chief who had steered the scheme through its legal and practical shoals; aged 53 and the scion of a wealthy family, he had been one of Abbey's first university recruits back in 1961.

Then there was John Bayliss, 55, a career-long Abbey man and the managing director heading the core home loans business, who had, during the pre-occupations of conversion, helped ensure that the group "kept its eye on the ball" of its normal activities. He had also shared in the PLC preparatory work, as had the slightly older John Ellis, also a long-time Abbey official, and - as the group's secretary - steeped in its history, procedures and culture.

With these were Peter Davis, non-executive deputy chairman, James Tyrrell, the finance director, Richard Baglin, the managing director in charge of new businesses, and a lately appointed executive board member, the former County NatWest chairman, Charles Villiers.

It was the most senior of these men who, with their non-executive board colleagues, had picked for Abbey National the pioneering course of a switch to company status, the transformation having being made possible by the Building Societies Act 1986. They had also shaped the changeover scheme designed to spread share-ownership of the new PLC widely and equally among the millions of members, who in turn had voted for it by a landslide.

The event was a landmark in money, investment and housing finance history for it showed that Abbey National, one of the UK's best-known names on the High Street, felt it had "come of age" and should assume the fresh mantle of banking status.

It was doing so as a group with more than £25 billion of the public's savings and more than £34 billion of mortgage and other assets, while its profits stood comparison with the average showing of some larger banks in the turbulent late-1980s. The group's 677-strong branch network, its growing Cornerstone estate agency chain and its near-10 million investment accounts gave it a strong base for growth in the field of financial services.

With the top Abbey team on the twenty-second floor of Kleinwort's Fenchurch Street skyscraper were their key advisers who for two years had also helped the group plan its way through the untrodden conversion path. Among them were Kleinwort's vice-chairman, Lord Rockley, a member of the aristocratic Cecil family, and his colleague, David Clementi, a director and veteran of giant privatisations like British Telecom's.

From Slaughter & May, the prominent City law firm which for many months had five partners involved almost full-time on the Abbey project, there was Nicholas Wilson - then one of Slaughter's leading men and now a top-flight National Westminster Bank adviser - and his younger colleague Tim Clark, who had worked at the heart of Abbey's conversion preparations.

Deloitte, the group's auditors who had played roles from reporting accountants to vote scrutineers, were represented by a senior partner, Roy Foster, and Peter Jeffrey, a senior manager who had also worked many months on the project. Others from Abbey's brokers, Rowe & Pitman (part of S. G. Warburg) and Kleinwort Benson Securities were also in the breakfastime party.

Two Bank of England people were also on hand, while the Stock Exchange manned the other end of an open telephone line. Lloyds Bank, as registrar and receiving bank for the big cash-raising issue, which had already been subscribed for, stood by to confirm that the money was held to Abbey's order.

Finally there were in attendance some of the younger Abbey men who had been most closely involved, notably Graeme Johnston, the conversion project co-ordinator, and Stewart Gowans, the corporate affairs manager.

The individual arrivals for this historic "Vesting Day," on which by 9 am Abbey National was to launch on its stock market career, were anxiously watched for. For that Wednesday was bedevilled, like others in the summer of 1989, by a rail strike.

This had meant more-than-normally careful preparations for the get-together to finalise the culmination of what had been billed "The Vote and the Float." Abbey drivers had set forth in the small hours to ferry top people to the meeting. At one point Peter Birch phoned in to report that he was caught in a Kew Bridge traffic jam,

A breakfast launch

while John Fry met hold-ups on his way in from Hertfordshire. As a precaution against non-arrival the Deloitte representatives each held a duplicate of a crucial document, while the Bank of England officials, who were due to bestow the banking licence without which neither conversion nor flotation could proceed, stayed overnight in London.

Before the croissants and champagne could be broached at a celebratory breakfast, however, vital final procedures had to be gone through. These were designed to unravel complexities discovered in the previously untried process of building society conversion.

Essential to the PLC's launch was the receipt of the banking licence. But the Bank of England could not hand over the licence until it was sure Abbey National PLC had enough capital to satisfy the exacting standards expected of banks.

Of this capital, £1.42 billion was accruing in the shape of the building society's reserves and £975 million more as cash put up against extra shares. Whether or not that issue could go "unconditional," the proceeds be gathered in and the underwriters freed of responsibility depended on the Stock Exchange granting listing ("a quote") for Abbey's shares. In its turn, the Stock Exchange needed assurance that the Bank's licence was forthcoming.

It was to let all these inter-dependent stages happen simultaneously that the Bank of England had agreed to be personally represented and the Stock Exchange to be in contact through an open line. But first, certain preliminaries had to be cleared out of the way by the assembled businessmen.

Earlier in the morning John Fry had formally assured Kleinwort's David Clementi that no last-minute disasters - such as the burning down of headquarters - had occurred overnight. This enabled a small board committee to declare that no new circumstances had arisen of the kind which would have obliged Abbey to publish fresh "listing particulars" before flotation could take place.

This is a fairly routine formality and proved to be so in this case. But it was only a few days previously that it had become clear that a very awkward hitch which could have blocked progress would not now in fact threaten the smooth completion of the whole exercise. For there had been an unusual provision in the cash issue's underwriting agreement that the whole transaction could be stopped on any legal appeal against the go-ahead previously given by the Building Societies Commission. A pressure group which had fought the PLC project had considered bringing such an action but had not in the end done so.

A breakfast launch

Next Deloitte, as auditors, certified that the issue money was to hand from Lloyds Bank and that the cash representing the reserves had been transferred in a cheque drawn by the building society on its account at the Bank of England.

Dated the previous evening. this historic piece of paper, one of the biggest cheques ever written, had read: "Pay to ABBEY NATIONAL PLC One Thousand Four Hundred and Twenty-Five Million Pounds Only. £1,425,000,000.00." It was signed on behalf of ABBEY NATIONAL BUILDING SOCIETY and had been "walked round" the Bank of England early that morning and stamped like the humblest cheque: PAID 12 JULY 1989.

With these and related formalities complete, the final stage had at last been reached.

Kleinwort's John Williams, a former Treasury man who had been closely linked with the conversion process, recalls the moment: "The Stock Exchange were saying, 'Right, we're ready to list. Have you got the banking licence?' The Bank said 'Yes' and we took its letter. Conditionality was broken and we were away."

The Bank's letter giving its licence (strictly speaking, authorisation under the Banking Act 1987) was handed over by the senior Bank official - and only woman executive - present, Ros Borer. The Stock Exchange posted its Rule 520 Notice adding Abbey National PLC's shares to its official list.

The Quote had - finally - followed the Vote and the Float.

At 9 am the high level party craned round screens as dealings began. The first quotation ticked over at 161p. Later in the day the price eased to 153p, a premium of 23p on the 130p cash offer price. This would have brought a member who had got the maximum 775 allotment on the cash issue a profit of some £300 if he had sold both his purchased and free shares.

There was an air of occasion as, the formalities complete, the most senior members of the party at last turned to their breakfast. Sir Campbell spoke appreciatively of what had been achieved and other leading players still recall their feelings on reaching the long-sought goal.

Slaughter's Tim Clark was struck by the brevity of the Bank and Exchange consents which everything had led up to: "That's what it was in the end: you'd done two years work for about six lines."

John Fry describes his own sensations as head of Abbey's conversion team: "A feeling of great relief. It looked as though it had got off at the right price - a key point for a new share issue. And one

A breakfast launch

really felt, at that stage, that one had actually finished."

The rueful tinge of this last sentence foreshadows the looming, but then, unsuspected, loss of many share certificates, the one disaster in an otherwise successful operation.

The celebration proved informal. Champagne was served but so stirred with excitement were those present that, as Nick Wilson puts it, ".... frankly, champagne was not necessary then." It is a house joke that Kleinwort's menu lacked the chairman's favourite marmalade.

Media attention was well in evidence. There are memories of TV cameras appearing over breakfasters' shoulders and tales of reporters being discouraged from invading the dealing room downstairs. By around 10 am the party had dispersed. Out at the grass roots, staff in Abbey's 770 branches received celebration cakes and new uniforms.

The story behind the use of the giant £1.42 billion cheque has already passed into Abbey folklore. At first the idea had been that the whole Abbey business would simply pass from society to PLC on vesting day at the stroke of a pen under a detailed agreement.

But a knotty problem arose in the hitherto untested conversion law. According to the legislation a converting building society had to create a claim on its starting reserves so that former savers, continuing as depositors, could receive something in the unlikely event of the new company going into liquidation. This entitlement, the so-called priority liquidation distribution, had to be secured under demanding conditions which, at one point, Abbey's planners could not see how to meet.

The problem, which was a potential "show stopper," was removed after Slaughter's Nick Wilson left a late meeting at Kleinwort's one night in February 1989 and went home to muse on the problem. While sipping whisky in his bath inspiration befriended him. At 3 am he rang his still-assembled colleagues to say: "I've cracked it."

He had hit on the solution that money must actually pass to establish the validity of the charge in the way required; hence the cheque. It was just one instance of the many novel problems needing to be solved in the long approach to conversion.

With the shares now safely featuring on dealers' screens, relief that Abbey National had successfully completed its transition to being Britain's fifth largest quoted bank was the greater given the long, arduous and problem-vexed nature of the course to conversion.

Planning and running the process had claimed hundreds of thousands of man-hours of high-powered effort, while repeated communications to millions of members needed hundreds of tons of paper and at times burdened the Post Office like a mini Christmas.

The new Abbey shareholder list of up to five million was Britain's largest, outsizing the three million-plus of TSB, the former Trustee Savings Banks, launched three years previously. The operation's cost, at £66 million, was less than first estimated and, while large, was smaller than TSB's £86 million.

In problems faced and mastered - including the lost share certificates, which for a time defeated the planners - Abbey's conversion/flotation exercise set up all sorts of records. It was after all the first trial of the radically new procedure created, in tune with the 1980s' deregulatory spirit, by the 1986 Act to let societies break out into the wider commercial sector.

Indeed, so complicated was the task that the 16 months from the board's March 1988 decision to recommend conversion to the project's achievement in July 1989 proved a very tight timetable. There was further work, too, through Abbey's introduction, in agreement with the Stock Exchange, of certain innovations over share application forms and certificates which became models for other mass issues like water privatisation.

The obstacle course of successive difficulties which loomed for Abbey's planners has been likened by John Fry, as team leader, to

Sir Campbell Adamson, 12 years Abbey National's chairman, who, while having an early leaning towards conversion, had to appear to be neutral while his board colleagues decided whether or not to cast off mutuality.

John Fry, one of Abbey's first university recruits who became the conversion team leader.

"scaling a mountain that has never before been climbed." Looking back, he recalls that "every time we reached what had looked like the summit, we would find that beyond it lay another peak waiting to be scaled."

Peter Davis, Abbey's finance expert who was part of the boardroom team which appointed Peter Birch as chief executive. He was given the job of second deputy chairman after fellow director Jeremy Rowe disagreed with the move to cast off mutual status. He then closed ranks so that the board could reach a unanimous decision.

The first and perhaps the most daunting crisis arose when, in January 1989, Abbey had unexpectedly to test its conversion scheme's legality in a "friendly" court case with its regulatory watchdog, the Building Societies Commission. After some nerve-tearing moments, the plan was endorsed by the chief Chancery Court Judge, the Vice-Chancellor, Sir Nicholas Browne-Wilkinson.

Next was "the Vote," the need for the PLC project to gain support from 75 per cent of Abbey's voting savers, 20 per cent of whom had to take part in the poll as well as a simple majority of

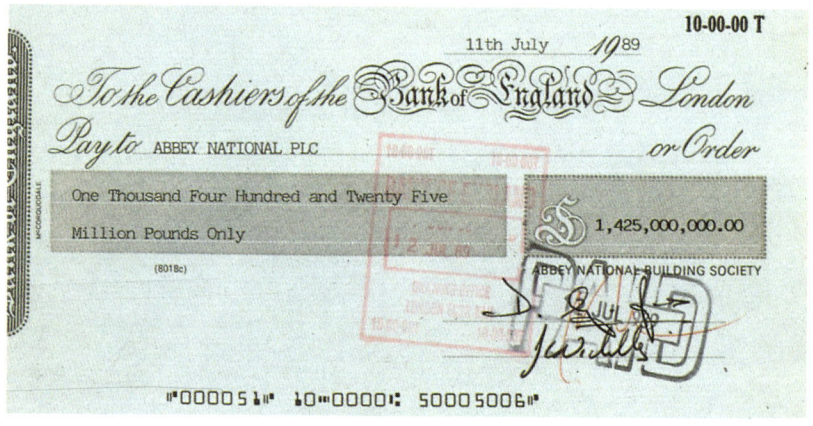

The £1,425,000,000.00 cheque, drawn on July 11, 1989, by Abbey National Building Society in favour of Abbey National PLC.

borrowers. The worry was that the legendary apathy of building society members might make it hard to reach the required savers' turnout.

The plan also met heavy attacks from the opposition group AMAF (Abbey Members Against Flotation) which, though ultimately unsuccessful, conducted a forceful campaign in the long British tradition of protest. Plentiful criticism surfaced, too, at the string of "road show" members' meetings, held by the chairman and chief executive around the country before the vote. The logistical arrangements for conducting the ballot - the largest-ever private poll in Britain - were immense.

The next big challenge was to secure the required approval for conversion from the Building Societies Commission. This procedure was a major one, involving a formal two-day public Confirmation Hearing, presided over by the BSC chairman Michael Bridgeman, at which most witnesses opposed the plan. Afterwards Abbey faced a worrying wait before the Commission confirmed the conversion, though requiring certain changes on children's entitlements and criticising Abbey for not more fully putting to members the case against its proposal. One commentator opined that it had consented "through gritted teeth." The Commission has since signalled it will require more time to consider any future conversions.

Abbey's National's final problem, and only major setback, occurred when, after conversion, some half a million share certificates went missing, many ending up burned in a South London skip. This episode much damaged the public perception of Abbey's conversion, though the disaster itself was quite quickly rectified.

Abbey National's move to separate itself from its fellow building societies by quitting the mutual ownership sector for a less restricted public company role was only embarked on after long and careful thought. The aim was to get more flexibility to diversify and raise capital in the competitive financial world of the late 20th Century, when growth in the traditional home loans business could be slowing. The matter was debated at a time when the building societies were being granted a much broadened operating framework.

Thus the issues addressed were complex and the study of them protracted. The Abbey board's unanimous conclusion to go for company status was not reached without doubts along the way and, in the case of one leading director, marked feelings of reservation. But, once made, the decision was followed through to success in a major and highly organised campaign which must stand as a classic of corporate effort and dedication.

By enabling millions to "unlock" much of their stake in Abbey National, the group's move poses queries whether other societies will follow suit and with what result, if they do, for the building society - and banking - sectors.

Whatever the future, Abbey National had come a long way in its ground-breaking strategy.

2

THE OLD ORDER CHANGES

IN THE upper part of Baker Street in central London's north-west postal district stands Abbey House, the home of Abbey National, one of Britain's largest financial groups with a long history of being in the public eye.

The headquarters is on the site of 221b Baker Street, known the world over as the mythical base of the celebrated 19th Century sleuth, Sherlock Holmes. A plaque by the entrance, which records this fact with a quote from "A Study in Scarlet" by Holmes' creator, Sir Arthur Conan-Doyle, is a popular focus with tourists from all over the world.

But Abbey National has persistently been in the news for reasons of fact, not fiction, and from long before it hit the headlines in 1989 for its pioneering switch to corporate status.

The group gained its name through a merger in 1944 of the UK's second biggest building society, Abbey Road - started in 1874 and with a name later given new fame by the Beatles - and the National Society, dating from 1840.

Although the National was the sixth largest society at the time, it had in the last century topped all rivals in size. One of its founders was the noted reformer Richard Cobden, who led a votes-for-all campaign and also successfully fought for the repeal in 1846 of the Corn Laws which had kept cheap foreign food from Britain's poor. One of Cobden's most cherished aims was to use the National to assist workers buy their homes and so win the vote, as property owners, under the prevailing restrictive franchise laws. In the event, Britain's electorate was widened by Acts of Parliament to include all adult males.

In this century, Abbey National has had further big names associated with it. A prominent chairman of Abbey Road before the merger was Josiah, later Lord, Stamp, whose granddaughter Elizabeth Stamp was one of conversion's opponents through the AMAF pressure group. Lord Hill of Luton, famed as the wartime "radio doctor" and afterwards a Conservative cabinet minister, chaired Abbey National from 1975 to 1978.

Abbey National's merger in 1944 proved a well-timed move, for it took place on the eve of a strong and sustained phase of growth for the building societies movement through the decades ahead. The societies, embodying a special "mutual" structure with no outside ownership, had their origins in the late-18th Century. The first societies were small groups which pooled money to build houses for their members, and then "terminated" when this was done. Later, in the 19th Century, as it was found that some participants wished to lend and others to borrow, the societies assumed a permanent character.

They were given a formal legal nature, with defined if limited objects, by the Building Societies Act 1874, the last radically new law in the field until the 1986 legislation which, among other changes, authorised conversion to company status.

In 1900 there were 2,286 societies, with £60 million assets between them. These figures had reduced to just 952 societies, but sharing £756 million assets, by 1940, when their savers numbered two million and their borrowers 1.5 million. Expansion in this post-war period from 1945 was more dramatic.

In the 35 years to 1980 the societies had total dominance of housing finance, and their loan and other assets leapt ahead to £54 billion, though mergers cut their number to 273. The reason the societies had the home loans arena so much to themselves was that the banks were effectively fenced off from entering the field by the lending curbs through which governments then helped influence the economy. Foreign financial groups were also excluded by exchange controls from playing in the UK market.

An implicit condition of this protected market was that the societies, which operated with a "cartel" of interest rates agreed through their "club," the Building Societies Association, endeavoured to keep these fixed rates as low as possible. Governments, mostly trying to combat inflation through policies of influence and persuasion, closely watched these rates and on one occasion paid a subsidy to prevent their rising. To fund their lending, the societies relied in essence on the thrift of individuals, to whom they appealed with such effect that by 1980 they had attracted nearly half the nation's personal short-term savings.

But, unlike the banks, they could not shop for cash in the cheaper City money markets. Competition between societies was thus not on price of loans but on quality of service and the brightness and availability of branches, whose numbers on the high streets trebled to 6,163 in the 11 years to 1981.

Despite the societies' successful expansion of their lending and savings-gathering - one result of which was a steady increase in the proportion of owner-occupation from 50 per cent to 55 per cent between 1970 and 1979 - a chronic mortgage shortage persisted. With tax breaks fuelling the desire for house buying, there was more underlying demand for home loans than could be met. Rationing was often needed and priority access to mortgages was frequently given to those saving with a society.

But all this changed with the election in 1979 of Margaret Thatcher's Conservative government and the gradual shift of world financial markets towards competition, de-regulation and less shutting off of sectors from each other. Before the end of that year exchange control on payments to and from abroad was scrapped after four decades and, in mid-1980, domestic loan controls were also removed from the big banks.

Thus, freed at last to compete in the enticingly safe and potentially lucrative mortgage market, the banks invaded it in strength and by 1981 had captured a 26 per cent share of new lending. Foreign financial groups were enabled by exchange control's abolition also to establish their toe-holds.

Faced with such rivalry, the societies had to look to their laurels. To defend their place in a mortgage market kept strong by pent-up demand, they had to shop more intensively for the funds principally open to them - the public's savings. Rates to savers were pushed up relative to general interest rates and it was obvious that mortgages would have to go the same way.

With the government now taking a hands-off attitude towards home loan rates, it obviously no longer made sense for the building society movement to stick to its cartel of fixed, and lowish, savings and mortgage rates. Little societies were already slipping the reins to woo funds and sell home loans at over-the-odds rates which hungry borrowers were happy to pay.

So it was not long before the big boys of the movement

followed suit. In November 1983, under Abbey National's lead, they scrapped the Building Societies Association's interest rate "cartel" and were liberated to set their own mortgage and savings rates as they wished.

The new situation of unfettered competition, with different financial sectors channelling in credit, produced an explosion of home loans business. Total net new mortgage lending multiplied from £7.3 billion in 1980 to £31.9 billion in 1988. With the former famine of loan supply over, unsatisfied demand proved to have been great. The seeming paradox of far more home loans being transacted at relatively loftier rates was explained by the release of the accumulated pressure to borrow. As the economic pundits put it, the market was cleared at a higher level.

Consequences included a climb in house prices, and a better deal than before for the societies' savers. Moreover the societies, like the banks, found their business paying well, since the buoyant market helped profit margins.

Yet the societies felt frustrated by their exclusion from wholesale money markets so heavily tapped by the banks and by their inability to follow their non-mutual rivals in raising share capital to underpin expansion. As the banks entrenched themselves in home loans, with a fluctuating new business share averaging 25 per cent, the societies were forced to ask "where do we go from here?"

This was the background to much role-reappraisal by the societies - and by Abbey National in particular - in the early 1980s. But the process occupied time.

The societies' priority was to win a widening of their permitted activities to obtain something nearer an even playing-field with their bank rivals. Under existing law, the societies were essentially confined to providing home-buyers with loans on first-mortgage and raising retail savings for the purpose, with little peripheral business permitted.

The banks, by contrast, could span a wide range of business. The societies also placed great importance on gaining access to the City's wholesale market as a supplement to their "retail" finance. After all, there was a limit to the extent to which they could afford to garner more personal savings by bidding up their price when the banks were more cheaply tapping the money markets pool.

It therefore became a major objective of the building societies from the early-1980s to persuade the government to give them a more flexible structure from which to compete with

The old order changes

rapidly diversifying rival financial institutions.

At the same time the concept of a building society taking the more radical course of transforming itself into a public company, thus gaining broader operational freedom, began to gain currency.

An important part of the background to this strategic discussion lay in developments in the United States among the savings and loan associations (S & L's or "thrifts"), the broad equivalent of British building societies. These bodies, like their UK counterparts, were essentially mutual bodies, with no owners other than their customers. There had long been a keen interest in switching various of them into stock (shareholder-owned) concerns.

A cartoonist's angle. Trog's view of how Abbey National was helping the disadvantaged through rundown housing renewal in the early 1980s.

From 1972, an earlier ban on the conversion of such associations into stock form was lifted. A notable case was when Citizens Federal Savings and Loan Association, a mutual body, became Citizens Savings and Loan Association, a stock company. This conversion was accomplished through the allocation of stock (the equivalent of UK shares) to the existing depositors of the concern, who thus became its owners.

However, conversions of this kind gave rise to fears that deposits would be transferred away from a converted concern to other mutuals in the hope of benefits when they, in turn, converted.

Such speculative flows did indeed develop and, from 1975, US regulations on the subject altered. The new rules provided that a converting body had to put its stock on sale at a price equal to its estimated worth, existing account-holders having priority rights to subscribe. Minimum voting levels to approve the deal were laid down, along with a 10 per cent limit on any shareholding within a year after conversion, as protection against a quick takeover.

Another requirement of the US system is that a liquidation account, equal to the existing reserves at the time of the changeover, should be set up on conversion. The idea of this "special reserve" is that savers with the former mutual who continue as depositors with the new stock group should have the right to receive benefits should the converted body be wound up. However, these rights are run down each time the depositor withdraws money, with the result that the liquidation account tends to decline to almost nothing within five years. As it does so, the pre-existing reserves steadily revert to being an unfettered part of the stock company's capital.

These American arrangements were to have considerable influence when Britain's law came to be rewritten to permit building societies to convert and when, later, Abbey National framed its own PLC scheme.

It should be noted that the later crisis which swept through the US S & L's had one key cause without parallel in Britain. This was that, while UK building societies normally lend and borrow from savers at adjustable interest rates, American S & L's had traditionally worked with fixed rates. Thus, when world interest levels jumped in 1979, S & L's were squeezed by having to buy funds more dearly without being able to raise revenues correspondingly. However, some of their troubles were also due to ill-chosen diversification.

These facts, like the US mechanisms of conversion, were very much in the minds of British ministers, officials and home loans chiefs when the UK building society law was updated.

While the idea of breaking out into the commercial sector gradually gained more building society attention, political thinkers were also focusing on the idea. A paper by Simon Mabey and Paul Tillett, published by the Conservative Bow Group in 1980, favoured legislation encouraging societies to change to company status.

Writing at a time when the interest cartel and other restrictions still made for inflexible markets, the authors felt that "many of these ills can be traced to the lack of any clear objective in a building society compared with the profit motive in an ordinary company." They saw "inefficiencies in the financial system which can only be satisfactorily rectified if the societies abandon their mutual status."

The writers believed that "although the building societies' transmutation should be voluntary, the advantages of it are sufficiently great that the Act should load the dice in favour of it happening rather than not happening."

Such radical ideas were not widely shared but formed part of the backdrop against which legislative plans eventually emerged. As to mechanisms of conversion, the paper noted the danger that free-share distributions might set off anticipatory speculative flows of deposits. But it envisaged share hand-outs for long-standing savers and perhaps for borrowers and staff as well.

Meanwhile, as such trends and thoughts developed throughout the financial world, important changes in top personnel and business were taking place in Abbey National.

What proved to be a turning point in the Abbey National story came in December 1975 with the sudden death - at only 62 - of its chairman, Sir Stanley Morton. Previously the society's chief general manager, Sir Stanley, a bluff, affable figure, was the latest among notable men who had led Abbey's strong growth in the post-war years. His predecessor (also his brother-in-law) was Sir Bruce Wycherley, while before them Sir Harold Bellman had been chairman of the combined group.

The unexpected loss of Stanley Morton left the board with the difficult and urgent problem of replacement, whose solution had far-reaching consequences. It was not made easier by the fact that the chief general manager, "Tim" Timberlake, was due to retire from his job in three years.

For their new chairman fellow-directors turned to the already quite elderly deputy chairman, Lord Hill who, after serving in the Cabinet, had in turn headed the Independent Broadcasting Authority and the BBC.

Then, in the course of 1976, the board received two notable recruits.

One was Jeremy Rowe deputy chairman and managing director (and afterwards chairman) of the London Brick group, whose family and business interests had long been in the field of housing and who was later to chair Peterborough Development Corporation. The other was Sir Campbell Adamson, an industrialist and holder of a number of public offices who was best known for the seven-year spell he had just served as director general of the Confederation of British Industry. Other directors on Abbey's board at this time included Lord Netherthorpe, once a director general of the National Farmers Union, and the chairmen of Abbey's advisory boards in Scotland, the north-west of England and Wales, respectively,

Sir John Carmichael, Sir Derek Hilton and Hugh Rees.

Within the next two years a surprise candidate was selected as Tim Timberlake's successor. This was Clive Thornton, Abbey National's chief solicitor who had formerly worked in the City; he was first appointed deputy chief general manager in 1978, becoming chief general manager soon afterwards. The choice upset prevailing expectations about the line of succession to the top executive post.

The tradition had been for one of the general managers to become chief and many had predicted that 44-year-old John Bayliss, one of the younger general managers, would get the post. Some old hands within the group described the selection from further down the pecking order of Clive Thornton - who was to have an innovating, high-profile and occasionally controversial five-year tenure - as "picking from the chorus line." But clearly the board wished to make a bold choice and one director of that time remarks that it was felt Clive Thornton had particular "flair."

His period in office was to be eventful and not without controversy.

The year 1978 brought a key fresh development when Lord Hill decided to retire and the need for a new chairman again arose. There were two obvious candidates, Sir Campbell Adamson, nationally known and with widely varied industrial and public experience, and the younger Jeremy Rowe, whose expertise was in the housing field with which Abbey's home loan activities had such an affinity.

There was some split of opinion among the directors but, of the two, each a graduate of Cambridge University, the board voted for Sir Campbell. Thanks to the good-humoured character of both men, the outcome was an amicable one. Jeremy Rowe became a deputy chairman in 1978, at first in tandem with Tim Timberlake but, after the latter was succeeded as chief general manager in 1979 by Clive Thornton, he was the sole deputy chairman.

In Sir Campbell Adamson, the society had gained a chairman with a natural gift for diplomacy and other qualities that were to prove highly relevant in the eventful years ahead. Aged 56 in 1978 and the son of a Scottish chartered accountant, he had first made his career in the steel industry, later becoming a director of various companies, including Imperial Group and Tarmac.

In the 1960s, when co-operation between business, labour and government was in fashion, he served two years as a top official in the Department of Economic Affairs under the Wilson Labour

The old order changes

government, next going on to run the Confederation of British Industry. His wide experience of public affairs had been filled out through membership of such bodies as the BBC advisory committee, the National Economic Development Council and the National Savings Committee.

With a reputation for balanced judgment and for being no ideologue, Sir Campbell, who lists "arguing" in "Who's Who" as a recreation, is a man who can understand different viewpoints. Indeed, during the general election campaign of February 1974, some remarks of his were regarded in right wing Conservative quarters as over-sympathetic to the Labour party's approach.

Of his role throughout the process of decision-making on Abbey's later conversion policy and its arduous implementation, one City adviser recalls: "The chairman had an incredibly important moderating influence."

Clive Thornton, Abbey's chief solicitor who rose to become chief general manager and then left to become chairman of Daily Mirror Newspapers. He gave Abbey a high profile but was never quite accepted by the building society world.

Another characteristic, his amiability, helped Sir Campbell handle members' meetings made stormy by anti-conversion protests, and smooth occasional moments of internal contention.

The new chairman came to his non-executive task at Abbey National - one involving several days a week, but not a management role - with broad, rather than long-standing building society experience. At the time and for a while afterwards, the surrounding environment was very different from what it was to become from the early 1980s.

Back in 1978 and into 1981, a year of urban unrest, the accent at the society was very much on meeting housing needs, particularly in rundown areas. In this trend Abbey's new chief general manager, Clive Thornton, who was becoming a live-wire generator of new ideas with a strong social conscience, was a powerful influence.

In 1980 Abbey National became the first society to release survey reports to borrowers and in the same year the society's share of the movement's assets grew to 16 per cent. Sir Campbell's address at the yearly meeting in April 1981 stressed the wide-ranging backing being given to the home buyer. "It is not our intention to offer the public an alternative, competing service to the one already provided by the High Street banks. Our business is housing - in all its forms - and our purpose is to give our members the most effective, efficient service available anywhere to help them fulfil all their housing ambitions. Our aims should not be too narrow."

Broader business initiatives followed one another; in 1981, the first advanced on-line counter terminals were installed in branches; 1982 brought the introduction of a seven-day savings account, followed a year later by the start of savings accounts with cheque books.

On the more social side, the society, then unable itself to go in for house-building, sponsored the Abbey Housing Association, to which it provided loans and know-how. It also took part in certain joint ventures which the government's inner cities minister, Michael Heseltine, wished to encourage. In the Stockbridge Village scheme it was associated with Barclays Bank and the local council in backing the renewal of a Liverpool housing estate. Abbey lent £3 million for this scheme: one director queried the suitability of such a substantial advance but it nevertheless went ahead.

In the first years of the 1980s the lineaments of the much altered new financial environment were growing clearer and Sir Campbell Adamson continued moves he had begun earlier to broaden Abbey's board and also to lower its average age. In line with what became general practice, 70 was established as the normal retirement age for directors; in the past some had stayed well into their eighties.

An early new appointee as a non-executive director in 1979 was the businesswoman Sara Morrison, then in her forties and now an executive director of GEC, who had been a vice chairman of the Conservative Party in the early 1970s. Two years later, the recently retired top Whitehall figure Sir John Garlick, who had been official chief of the Department of the Environment, the government department concerned with building societies, joined the board.

So did Sir Edward Singleton, a leading solicitor and former

The old order changes

chairman of the Law Society. In 1982, the younger Peter Davis, a chartered accountant who was then deputy chairman of the Harris Queensway store group, and now finance director of the Sturge Holdings financial group, became a non-executive director.

Another board recruit in 1984 was Dame Jennifer Jenkins, then a director of Sainsburys, who is the wife of Lord (Roy) Jenkins, a former Chancellor of the Exchequer and President of the European Commission. In 1981, Sir Iain Tennant and Sir Myles Humphreys, who respectively headed Abbey National's advisory boards in Scotland and Northern Ireland, also joined the main board.

At this time, the only full-timer to be a director was Clive Thornton, who had been so appointed a year after becoming chief general manager.

John Bayliss. As managing director of the home loans business, he ensured that Abbey did not distract itself from its core activities while the preparations for conversion and flotation were underway.

A year later a significant full-time appointment at general manager level was that of the chartered accountant James Tyrrell who came from the world of commerce and who quickly introduced more detailed financial reporting.

By various accounts, board meetings of building societies had, in earlier decades, sometimes been brief, even rubber-stamping, affairs. On the other hand, the Abbey National board, as it took shape in the first half of the 1980s, had - as one of its then new members recalls - been "strengthened and widened with people who thought they might have a view about things." This seems latterly to have led to occasional brushes with the chief general manager, a man of strong and decided views whose relations with his management colleagues also appear to have had their moments of tension.

Around the end of 1983 Clive Thornton decided, after five

years as management chief, to leave to become chairman of Daily Mirror Newspapers, this being not long before the unexpected takeover of the Mirror Group by Robert Maxwell's interests.

As a dynamic manager - "he would spin off 10 ideas, three good," a critic remarks - Clive Thornton may not have been an always comfortable colleague but was respected for his creativeness and energy. His commitment to the causes of housing and of the disadvantaged also gained him appreciation, while his attention to press relations ensured extensive coverage of Abbey developments.

James Tyrrell, Abbey's business-minded finance director who lead the task force to deal with financial planning.

A friendly observer remarks: "Clive Thornton was a controversial figure but he gave a tremendous impetus to Abbey, put it in the situation where it was seen as the most progressive and expanding society. It is a pity he was never accepted by the building society world." Leaving for a new field and much younger than the traditional chief general manager departing at retirement age, he was not invited to stay on the board as his predecessors generally had been.

The need to appoint a new management chief now confronted the board with what was to be an exceptionally important decision, coming as it did just after the cartel's scrapping had positioned the societies to play more freely in a competitive environment. Elsewhere in the financial world, deregulation was underway too: plans were already afoot for the major "Big Bang" shakeup in the Stock Exchange.

Speaking of this time and of the board's continuing objective of toning the group up for the fresh era, Sir Campbell recalls: "We saw that the whole cosy thing was coming to an end. Clive Thornton had seen it as well. It wasn't going to, it couldn't, go on. We knew that Big Bang was coming. And when we moved to break the cartel, it was very deliberately done, because we thought that would be the start of sharpening us up, as much as anything else. We knew that ours would then be a rather more sophisticated, rather less simple, business than it had been before."

As it also happened, the board approached the crucial choice of a new chief executive when clear prospects were opening of new powers for building societies.

3

A NEW LAW AND A NEW BOSS

FACED with the change sweeping the financial world, the building societies had soon set to work to consider the reforms needed to update their antiquated legal framework for an age in which the largest were on a par with the top banks. Their essential aim was to be placed on a more even footing with other financial institutions.

In mid-1981 the Building Societies Association (BSA) established a group, chaired by John Spalding, chief general manager of the Halifax, the biggest society, to review the societies' constitution and powers and the law governing them. Public discussion was opened up in a BSA paper early in 1983, followed by final proposals a year later.

These recommended that societies, while retaining their basic character as mortgage providers, should be allowed to undertake a wider range of new functions related to their mainstream business. In particular, they should be able to branch out into connected services like estate agency and conveyancing, supply limited personal and other additional loans, and provide certain retail banking facilities, including cheque books, credit cards and cash dispensers. Among other changes called for through a modernised law was the creation of power to hold land for development and to operate in other European Community countries. A considerable part in the preparation of the proposals was played by Mark Boleat, then deputy director-general, now director-general of the Building Societies Association and one of Britain's leading experts on the industry.

At the same time it was proposed that societies which wished to do so should be able to convert to company form from the mutual status which the industry generally would retain.

These ideas found a receptive hearing in government circles. In its 1983 general election manifesto, the Conservative Party promised early public consultation on how the societies could play a fuller part in providing people with new housing and on how to bring the law up to date. A Green Paper outlining the government's approach was issued in July 1984 and a Bill was published in December 1985. The "conversion" clauses were filled out later, after a special consultation process based on a Treasury paper.

The conversion clauses attracted controversy since the Labour Party opposed the provision for a conversion option. Attachment to the mutual ethos ensured much questioning of the concept of a change to bank status for any building society.

This was reflected in lively debates in both Houses of Parliament - Labour strongly pressing its opposition on all occasions - and the Bill finally became law as the Building Societies Act 1986 on July 25 1986.

The Act, which gave the societies the great part of what they wanted, and was worked out under the close supervision of Ian Stewart, MP, the Economic Secretary to the Treasury, had a number of special features.

As well as being enabled to perform mortgage-linked functions like conveyancing, the societies were empowered to lend more widely, to provide cheque books and related services, and to operate in fields including insurance broking, unit trusts and pension provision. To their great relief, they were also enabled to tap the wholesale money markets for funds, at first up to 20 per cent, and later 40 per cent, of their requirements.

The societies were in addition given the right to hold land for residential building development and to operate, through subsidiary companies, in other states of the European Community. However, the new law did not confer the power, which some societies had wanted, to own or acquire a bank.

It was a key aspect of the Act that, to a substantial extent, it allowed increased operational scope to be granted to societies by government order (secondary legislation) as time went on. For instance, the power to conduct broader banking, stock-broking and trustee and executor services was conferred in 1988. The ratios of the three classes into which the Act divided commercial assets - first mortgages for home buyers, other property lending, and personal loans and certain investments - were adjustable too.

The initial minimum for first mortgages would thus fall from a starting 90 per cent to 75 per cent by 1993 but could not drop further. The maximum for personal loans was doubled to £10,000.

Flexible as the Act is, however, it sets certain bounds to the extent to which proportions of business can be adjusted. For example no subordinated legislation can reduce below 75 per cent the proportion of a society's commercial assets which are held as first mortgages. Equally, a society may not raise more than 40 per cent of its funding in wholesale form. These constraints are known as "nature limits," the idea being that without them building societies would no longer truly be building societies.

The pattern of adjustable limits reflected the government's wish to monitor closely how the reform package was working out. The concept of the three classes of loans was very much the personal brainchild of Ian Stewart, to whom the Chancellor, Nigel Lawson, delegated authority to handle the Act. Stewart who, as a former merchant banker, is a specialist in City matters, also paid special attention to the conversion provisions.

In its Green Paper of July 1984 foreshadowing the Act, the government rejected the radical suggestions sometimes made that societies should be encouraged - or even forced - to change into public companies. "A compulsory change to company status has been advocated by some in the past on the grounds that their mutual constitution insulates societies from the effects of competition, leaving too much scope for inefficiency and extravagance in their managements," the paper stated. But it added that the government "does not accept that such a change is needed."

However, the paper went on to explain that "it is wrong that a society cannot turn itself into a company if its members so wish .... Although there are no signs that many societies will wish to become companies in the near future, this will provide greater flexibility... It would also provide a means by which a society which wished to diversify radically could acquire the necessary increase in its capital base reasonably quickly."

It was also explained that conversion plans would need approval by societies' members and that, after the changeover, the successor company would need licensing by the Bank of England.

In the first public indication in Britain of the mechanism by which ownership of a building society might change hands, the paper envisaged that conversion would generally involve "a scrip [free] issue of company shares to existing shareholders [savers] with holdings above a certain threshold, with the conversion of existing shares [savings] into deposits, and the issue of further shares, by a rights issue or otherwise, to secure additional capital."

These indications led to a good deal of discussion, and some differences of view, on conversion procedures within the building society movement over the next year and a half. The result was that the Treasury's consultative paper about the method of conversion was less clear-cut on the subject of free shares than the Green Paper. It warned against the dangers of immediate share hand-outs as perhaps prompting conversions which would lead to quick takeovers, with destabilising consequences.

Instead, the paper canvassed the procedure of a society converting through a public offer of shares, with priority rights for its own savers to subscribe (the US model later followed in the flotation of the formerly mutual TSB). The concept of phased bonus share issues to savers of, perhaps, two years' standing, was included as well.

These ideas received a somewhat lukewarm reception from the Building Societies Association, which rather favoured an American-style "liquidation account" to be held against the reserves taken over on conversion until all previous members' rights on them had expired. Abbey National's own response included a plea that the conversion procedure should be as flexible as possible.

Other proposals by the Treasury included an anti-takeover "protective provision" barring any individual share stake in a converted company from exceeding 15 per cent during the first five years. As to approval by members, the plan was that a society's conversion was to require 75 per cent backing from savers, at least 20 per cent of whom had to vote, and support from a simple majority of borrowers.

The conversion parts of the Bill, and of the Act, followed these latter provisions. On the mechanism of conversion, the Act was vaguer than the Treasury paper. It did not exclude share benefits being given as part of the transformation process, but laid down that, where a converting society's members received "rights to acquire shares in priority to other subscribers," this entitlement should be confined to savers of at least two years' standing. This aspect of the Act was often later criticised as obscure and unclear.

Provision was also made for a "priority liquidation distribution," evidently modelled on US practice. It was stipulated in addition that the societies' members able to vote on a conversion scheme should exclude savers with under £100 and minors.

Conversions would need "confirmation" by the Building Societies Commission, the new reinforced watchdog regulator of societies which was taking over from the Registry of Friendly Societies.

In the Parliamentary debates, the new power for building societies to convert was not only opposed by the Labour Party but criticised by some Conservatives as well. Fears were expressed that the commitment to housing finance would decline, that multinationals would buy up converted societies and that Britain would have too many clearing banks.

Ian Stewart, piloting the Bill, stoutly defended the right to convert, but insisted that it should not "be an easy option." There was no significant Parliamentary debate on the mechanisms of conversion.

Stewart later explained: "I became very concerned about the way ahead for the building societies. It seemed essential to let them branch out or they would be increasingly at a disadvantage vis-a-vis the banks and the TSBs."

He envisaged that much transformation might take place over a longish spell of years, but did not want a spate of quick change. The reasons included the "gulf of culture" between the top societies and small ones, the latter's lack of management skills necessary for launching into complex commercial banking and the intolerable burden that numerous conversions could place on the banking supervision system. There was also the danger of triggering a spate of stock market bids for newly converted societies.

"I thought what was needed was a period of gradualism, in which societies would extend and develop. On the other hand, it seemed wrong to constrain the big societies from moving closer towards general banking if the managements and members wanted this," Stewart said.

"So I was quite satisfied we needed a provision allowing societies to convert into PLCs. Otherwise we would be imposing a potentially unnatural constraint on the large societies for a number of years."

At the same time, he did not wish to see a high proportion of the societies by volume changed into banks soon after the new law. "Then you would no longer have had a building society movement. I didn't want the consequence of the new Act to be such a cataclysm of change. Nor should the conversion process be unduly easy.

"My view was that it was a major step to become a PLC and shouldn't be undertaken unless a society felt impelled to do it because it had a sense of being in a strait-jacket which it wanted to get out of."

One of the most contentious conversion provisions in the Act was that at least 20 per cent of all qualified savers had to vote on a proposal to convert, a 75 per cent minimum of those taking part having to be in favour. Support from a simple majority of borrowers, balloted separately, was also required. Feeling in the societies in the mid-1980s was that, given past voting inertia, a 20 per cent turnout was an unattainable "threshold," so that in insisting on it, the government was effectively taking away with one hand the conversion opportunity it gave with the other.

The BSA, Abbey National and others lobbied hard, but in vain, for easier rules in the Act. Stewart was adamant, even at one time considering a still higher voting requirement.

He later explained: "If societies couldn't rally that number (20 per cent), they couldn't demonstrate to me that it was the overwhelming wish of the membership to change its status. It seemed to me that an essential part of the process was the democratic participation by members. If a society couldn't organise that, they weren't doing the job I expected of them."

Ian Stewart, MP, the economic Secretary to the Treasury. He was delegated to handle the new building society legislation's passage through parliament by the Chancellor, Nigel Lawson.

As to Abbey's experience, the minister, who later became a privy councillor, said: "It's a long and gradual process for a business to change. I always expected Abbey would attempt conversion first and be successful. But I didn't want them to saunter it."

Of later events, he added: "I think I was surprised that the eventual 'pro' vote was so high, but I expected the society to clear the hurdle comfortably - and it did!"

It was before this process of modernising the building

societies law was complete that Abbey National selected its new chief executive. Indeed the appointment was made before the government's outline of its own legislative plan and when ample time remained for commenting, as Abbey did, on the conversion provisions. The man chosen was Peter Birch, who was picked from a business background and, as it happened, was an early proponent of conversion.

This choice proved crucial for later developments and was in, fact, intended by the board to be a landmark in the group's evolution.

In a break with past practice, the directors opted to seek and consider outside candidates, with head-hunters Goddard Kay Rogers given the search task.

Internal candidates - and there were good ones - stood as possibles. But the mere fact that the net was so deliberately cast beyond the society tipped the probability towards a non-Abbey recruit. A new type of boss for a new era seemed what the board wanted.

Peter Davis, the present deputy chairman and himself then a 43-year old businessman and a relatively new non-executive recruit to the board, sums up the thinking: "The recent breaking of the cartel was a major decision that perhaps set the tone and indicated the context in which we were working. We had always been rather the 'enfant terrible' of the industry - the aggressive bloody nuisance in the eyes of the movement, if you like - which we thought a compliment. Now we felt, in view of the environment we were operating in, and of the way it was likely to go in future, that we were going to be better off having an outsider rather than a true-blue dyed-in-the-wool building society man."

Davis' words on Abbey's image tally interestingly with some long-standing general views of the group as the big society with a name for being metropolitanly streetwise, innovative and awkwardly different on occasions. The appraisal perhaps helps explain how the group's most radical move ever - its conversion - was able to grow out of its own culture.

External candidates were whittled down to two and the board, through a sub-committee for the purpose, also considered one or two internal candidates from among the general managers destined to play their own major future roles. Eventually, the directors decided to follow through the idea of an external appointment.

In the event they chose Peter Birch, then aged 47, managing director of the American-controlled razor blade company Gillette (UK) and a recognised marketing expert. Sir Campbell Adamson later spoke of his own role in the selection as "probably the most important task a chairman ever does in an institution."

One other director singles out the policy at this time as the first decisive turn down the road of Abbey National's transformation into PLC form. "When we decided not to appoint a traditional building society chief executive, but to go to the market place for a man with a broader commercial experience from outside the movement, I think that at that stage the course was set for conversion."

Sir Campbell has his own way of expressing the position as he recalls a talk, before the appointment, with the future chief executive who, at that time, "didn't know, as I didn't know when I came, a building society from a hole in the ground."

In that conversation, the chairman remembers: "I said: Now, Peter, you're at Gillette and you're in the ordinary market economy. You may think this is a fairly simple business, but it's all going to change. And there seems quite a strong possibility that going PLC may be allowed under the coming new Building Societies Act. The thing that to me is important, as chairman, is that if you take this job, you should be looking to get our management organised, whether we go PLC or not. It's a changed world and we want a much stronger and better outside mix with the inside building society people than we've had before.'

"It didn't much matter at that time whether we were going PLC or not. What mattered was that the world was going to change and we had to start behaving rather differently - in a whole series of market terms and profit terms and everything else. And Peter - it was one of the main reasons he was chosen - was just the man to do that. That was his background."

One significant change from the moment Peter Birch took over in April 1984 was in his title. He was appointed "chief executive," a name more redolent of the commercial world than the former style of "chief general manager."

In another break with earlier practice, he was also at once made a director; and within three months two senior general managers, John Bayliss and John Fry, also joined him on the board. These full-time board appointments were in tune with what had become established practice among the big banks. Other senior executives also became directors in due course.

Peter Birch remembers the brief he was given for his new job: "The remit from Sir Campbell to me was to position Abbey National soundly and securely for whatever changes might take place in the

A new law and a new boss

future. I think we set about doing that." By common consent, his arrival was viewed as a sea change.

The new chief executive is a slender, athletic figure, sometimes thought a little unbending despite an amicable manner. Previously nurtured in the world of major multinationals, he had gone straight from school and National Service to seven years with Nestle before joining Gillette, so he came to Abbey National with long experience of running international businesses.

Many of his initiatives, which were to make Abbey National more commercial, reflect his previous experience. While a delegator - John Bayliss is, for instance, very much left to run the traditional and major home loans side of the group - Peter Birch is an active chief manager, who has introduced many new business methods and is also an alert cost-watcher. One non-executive director says of him: "He's extremely tough and determined. He's mean in the sense that he controls expenses very tightly."

Peter Birch, Abbey's chief executive. He was brought in from Gillette (UK) to "commercialise" the mutual and played a key role in the decision to convert to PLC status.

Birch's firm hand all round on costs - as a tiny example, Abbey sent no Christmas cards in its first year as a PLC - has contributed to the group's relatively low ratio of costs to revenue. In 1987, this was 45.2 per cent, compared with well over 60 per cent at the big four High Street banks.

As to his reaction on being approached about possibly joining Abbey, Birch, who had been with Gillette for 19 years with more than 12 of these as a general manager or managing director, recalls at first saying he was very happy where he was.

"But then I thought, life is full of challenges and it sounded an extremely interesting opportunity. And I suppose I was very flattered to be offered the chance of joining Abbey National." He keeps in touch with other business sectors through some non-executive directorships, including ones at Hoskyns and Argos.

One earlier experience which casts some light on the new chief executive's personality concerns his National Service in the Army in the mid-1950s. While most of those leaving Eton Hall Cadet School after their subaltern's training opted for a British regiment, Birch gave his preference to three forces further afield - the Jamaica Regiment, the Somaliland Scouts and the Mauritius Militia.

"I thought, well I'm only a National Serviceman, and I might as well do everything I can." He became a Second-Lieutenant in the Jamaica Regiment.

In Jamaica, then still a British colony, he shared a room with another young officer, Kenneth Barnes. Later, after independence, Ken Barnes became one of the chiefs of the Jamaica Defence Force and is the father of John Barnes, the celebrated Liverpool soccer star. Peter and Gillian Birch keep in touch with Ken Barnes and his wife Jean and have, in recent years, stayed with them in Jamaica. This link illustrates another side of his personality in addition to the impression he sometimes gives of being a narrowly-focused businessman.

Of his arrival at Abbey National, Peter Birch later remembered: "My initial impressions were that here was an organisation with an incredibly good brand name that stood for confidence, security and all the good things in life - with a management team that was very long in experience in the building society world.

"I think that, when one goes into an organisation, one can tell what sort of organisation it is through the culture of the people. There was a feeling of pride within the management team. I think they were obviously suspicious of a newcomer joining. But they seemed to be saying: 'We'll give you a chance but you'll have to prove yourself.' They were very friendly and really welcomed me and bent over backwards to try and help me understand the situation here."

One early development was the creation of a new strategy group. This is a forum in which four or five times a year Abbey National's seven or eight top executives spend a day or two away from the office discussing future policy with a formal agenda. In this setting has originated the thinking on many developments, above all the plan for taking Abbey into the company sector.

"From that group has come everything that's happened within the organisation," Birch comments.

As to the more general management approach he presided over from 1984, he adds: "We settled down as a management team with some very clear objectives, which we rapidly developed. Important among those was the need to be financially sounder than other organisation. We saw ourselves doing that through being prudent, building up reserves and keeping our overheads low. That was the platform for wherever we were going."

In line with this more commercial orientation there were further improvements in the flow of financial information, including monthly reporting on how income and spending was going in relation to a budget looking five years ahead and reflecting strategic planning. Terminology altered from "surpluses" which, Peter Birch says, "I likened to things choirboys wear," to "profits." It was to be another three years before Abbey's published yearly financial statements fully blossomed forth in a new format as company-style Annual Accounts.

Further changes in the personnel field emphasised the executive's resolve to update Abbey National's culture in response to the more competitive environment.

One was a shift from the former practice of giving all-round cost-of-living pay rises to a more performance-related remuneration system, based on a "management by objectives" programme. Under this everybody in the organisation set objectives for themselves in discussion with their immediate boss. Then, during the year and at the year-end, each staff member sits down formally with his or her manager and reviews performance against the objectives.

From this comes a rating according to a scale of merit. The salary increase is then fixed by reference to the individual's showing on a five-point scale which ranges from "exceptional" through "highly effective" and "effective" down to "less than effective" and "unacceptable." The individual, as well as the manager, signs the resultant report, which then needs approval by the manager's own boss.

Peter Birch, who sees all the results, explains that Abbey National expects to see rather more than 60 per cent of staff in the middle "effective" grade. Perhaps 15 per cent rank as "highly effective" and an elite five per cent as "exceptional." From these latter two classes, top management picks out likely "flyers" and aims to plot their future career path.

Training has been a further matter stressed under the new

regime. Staff from general manager to branch manager have attended short-term training courses run by the Management Centre Europe organisation. The arrangement assists staff to take a step back from their business and look at it from outside.

"I believe the training programmes were very helpful in broadening people and giving them different perceptions," Birch says. Another innovation was a profit-sharing scheme for all employees.

Terence Murphy, the general manager who headed Abbey National's personnel side for a few years until 1988, has written about the importance of training in the executive's drive to modernise the society's culture after 1984.

In an article in 1989 Murphy, who was by then become a partner in the Murphy Miller Ginsburg human resources consultancy, spoke of the aim to "change the style and behaviour of managers at all levels from the autocratic and paternalistic to one that could be described as management by consent." He records that about 150 managers who were not comfortable with the new approach left with generous early retirement and redundancy packages. Nonetheless, there appears to have been some internal controversy about that shakeup, some people considering that the departure of such a considerable number of mainly older managers was too radical.

While the first of these and other developments towards positioning Abbey National for its future role were under way in 1984, the idea of building societies switching to company status was already a talking point in the financial world, although the Building Societies Act still lay in the future. The chairman remembers Peter Birch coming into his office one day and saying: "You know, Campbell, I'm absolutely convinced we should become a PLC."

It was the beginning of how that course was chosen by Abbey National's top managers as the right one for their group.

4

TO BE, OR NOT TO BE, A PLC

THE management team which first faced the "PLC or mutual?" choice in 1984 consisted of the recently reshaped top management which, with later additions, was to run Abbey National for years to come. With varied backgrounds, the six-strong group had an average age of no more than forty-nine and was gradually to reason its way to agreement in favour of a switch to corporate and bank status.

Heading it was the slight, determined figure of Peter Birch, who had recently arrived from the world of business - and of US-style management methods. Of the two senior colleagues who had joined him on the board, the older was John Bayliss, a man of vast experience in the group, which he had joined in 1957. With a laconic wit and good humour, he would probably have been ultimately cast for the leading management role had Abbey's succession line worked out as planned in the mid-1970s. As it is, Bayliss holds a key position in today's more diversified Abbey National as managing director of the mainstream building society business and has no lament that the group has evolved along new courses.

Also a director as well as a general manager was John Fry, over 20 years with Abbey National but who had arrived through a slightly different route from that of the society's traditional talented school-leaver recruit. He was to be of central importance to the conversion programme, being given responsibility for leading the complex operation.

As his middle name records, John Marshall Fry is a sprig of a family which owns one of Britain's biggest private companies, the Marshalls of Cambridge aircraft, engineering and garage group headed, until lately, by his uncle, Sir Arthur Marshall. Marshalls is the firm which, among other defence inventions, devised special in-flight refuelling techniques for the Falklands War.

John Fry took a law degree at Cambridge, then worked for two years in the family business learning to fly and working petrol pumps. The prospect of a spell of years on the garage side then caused him to doubt if this was the career for him.

His decision to switch to something different perhaps enjoyed inspiration from on high, for he was advised by his old Cambridge tutor, the future Archbishop of Canterbury, Dr Robert Runcie, then Dean of Trinity Hall. Fry joined Abbey National as only the second university graduate the society had taken on. An outside adviser on the conversion later spoke of John Fry's patience, dedication and willingness to concern himself in detail during the coming PLC marathon, saying "he attracted enormous loyalty. He was very fair, very calm under pressure."

Another general manager was John Ellis, who had been secretary to the society since 1979. Concerned in that capacity with board business and with Abbey's legal and other rules, he is sometimes referred to by the chairman as "the keeper of my conscience." Often seen as a traditional building society man, Ellis was an early enthusiast for conversion. The jealous guardian of the society's procedures, he was later to face Abbey's need, during the PLC process, to be guided to an unprecedented degree by specialist outside advisers.

Rather younger than their colleagues were two other general managers. One was Richard Baglin, who had joined Abbey National in his early 20s and who, from 1986, was to steer the expansion of new business ventures, including the estate agency chain. The other was James Tyrrell, a chartered accountant of buoyant manner and a business-minded approach, who had been recruited from EMI to head the finance side. These two later joined the group board, respectively in 1988 and 1989. In 1986 there were two other general managers, Charlie Toner, who was to be responsible for the branch network which he still heads, and Terence Murphy, who ran the personnel side but left Abbey National in 1988.

Colleagues recall that Peter Birch, in the way of those bringing a fresh eye to a scene, quickly started asking fundamental questions and querying certain time-honoured assumptions. "What is the value of mutuals?" and "why haven't we got a profit motive here?" were typical.

This was a time when the building society movement was

reeling somewhat from the bankers' drive into the home-loans market. So strong had this been that the societies' share of new mortgage lending had been cut to 57.6 per cent in 1982 from 78 per cent in 1980. Although the banks pulled back somewhat in the next few years, they were to renew their incursion more strongly in 1987.

Such a background was one against which societies came increasingly to protect their position by watching profitability, since growth of lending could no longer be exclusively relied on for profit. Under its new regime Abbey National was prominent in this trend, costs being closely vetted and loans of risky character more closely scrutinised.

John Fry recalls: "The organisation changed under Peter Birch's direction to become much more focused on profit, which was a tremendous advantage to us. It meant we were ahead of the game when the coming Act, by broadening building society activities, required higher capital ratios - and therefore all societies had to turn more to profit."

John Ellis puts it this way: "In the past, building societies grew and grew. But as competition became greater and the mortgage market began to reach further towards maturity, growth could no longer be the primary objective. So the emphasis switched more to profitability and that was about the time Peter joined us."

The banks' appearance on the societies' once protected home-loans patch was also highly relevant to thinking on the inevitably more complex and long-term question of whether a future opportunity to convert should be seized. A good deal of City commentary in 1984 through to 1986 was painting the sombre scenario that the societies faced a permanently reduced share of their "one-product" mortgage market, whose overall growth might also be slowing for population and economic reasons.

This further prompted the Abbey National management team to question how well their group could survive as a mutual, unable to diversify beyond the limited range of activities open to building societies. The urgency with which it appraised the matter was increased by widespread predictions that the mortgage market might indeed be approaching a "mature" phase, affording little room for growth.

That this reassessment had already got under way five years before the change to PLC status in mid-1989 is clear from the group's records. In July 1986, John Fry told directors in a preliminary submission on the subject: "The General Managers' Strategy Group have spent a great deal of time considering this [the conversion] issue over the past two years."

The management proceeded in 1985 to consult a City analyst John Tyce, of Laing & Cruickshank, who was an acknowledged specialist in the field of banking and finance. His assessment was not encouraging about the prospects for long-term future operations in unchanged form as a mutual. The boost competition was giving to the cost of winning savers' cash, and the prospect of more new mortgage lenders capturing business, could affect profitability, he warned, while squeezed earnings would restrict capital to support growth. Such pressures could not be counted on to be offset by one favourable factor, the expected ability to tap City money markets for cheaper funds.

In more detail, there was the prospect that the costs of retail money would continue to rise in the years ahead as savers, already wooed with better interest, switched more cash from lower to higher yielding accounts. The competitive environment in which the tussle for retail funds had already taken hold was set to continue and to foster the trend.

So far, societies had done much to resist the consequent pressures on their profit margins by means of cost cuts and such devices as premium interest rates on large mortgages. But there was a warning (which proved correct) that such over-the-odds rates on big loans would prove hard to sustain.

At the same time the new, more barrier-free structure of the financial industry was likely to draw fresh types of lenders into the mortgage market, and enhance the threat from recent entrants, further boosting the competition societies faced. In particular, there were signs of foreign banks piling in as lenders, while insurance groups also sought to make loans as an aid to selling their main wares.

In addition, Britain could (though it might not) see the growth of a US-style securitised mortgage market, under which investing institutions would buy up mortgages for their own portfolios, so refunding the main mortgage lenders to advance cash afresh and further increasing competition.

At best, if a building society's profitability on its home-loans business could, one way or another, be held at its existing level, it should be possible for the mutual body to hold its market share. However, its scope for diversification could be limited compared with that of a rival with access to outside capital. A no-growth scenario could, in fact, be the outlook.

On the other hand, a switch to company status would allow

the converted group to raise substantial share capital, enhancing its competitive power in the mortgage market by comparison with societies staying mutual and its ability to diversify. It would also permit acquisitions against the issue of shares and enable the business to give senior management incentives through share options.

The persuasive arguments of this report in favour of conversion had considerable impact on Abbey's management, coinciding as they did with other City studies highlighting the societies' prospective problems in the more open financial setting.

Yet at least one member of the executive, John Fry, had not been quickly won over to the case for conversion. Fry recalls a Strategy Group meeting at a time when there had been "a lot of talk of Armageddon coming round the corner."

At this gathering, he said to his colleagues, who were largely already persuaded with varying degrees of enthusiasm: "Hold on a moment. You're all saying we ought to convert and that there are good reasons for it. But nobody's actually examined the case for remaining mutual."

He recalls, with a twinkle, Peter Birch then saying to him - "rather like Henry II, of Archbishop Thomas a Becket, 'who will rid me of this turbulent priest?' - Well, if you feel like that, John, go away and make the case."

What the society did was to call in independent consultants, John Kitching Associates, whose brief was to carry out an objective assessment of the PLC option and assess the viability of the alternative of remaining mutual. The consultants spent time at Abbey House from mid-November 1985. An interim report was presented orally in early January 1986 and a written report, taking account of points then raised, delivered later that month.

In essence, the conclusion was that while the society, by staying mutual, might, despite the pressures and given certain action, manage to expand further, it could expect to do better, achieving faster growth rates, as a PLC. This, it was argued, was because, being then positioned with more capital, it would be able to gain market share, carve out a good slice of the newly-opened unsecured personal loan market and perhaps take over other societies. The point was also made that, if Abbey did not convert, a rival society might do so and itself reap these advantages.

The study took as its starting point that Abbey National aimed at sustained, profitable growth, from a secure and strengthening base and in conditions calculated to nourish motivation and commitment among the staff. It was more optimistic than the earlier report on the chances of further expansion for a group like Abbey National in continued mutual form. This view was founded on the fact that the worst effects of the tussle for savings and of other competition had already been absorbed and that societies would, under the new Act, be able to fight the banks on their own ground by creating a lucrative personal loans business. Thus, some profitable growth would, with the aid of various particular adjustments, still await an Abbey National of unaltered structure.

However, these future growth prospects could be improved radically further were the group to get access to the substantial extra equity (share) capital a switch to PLC form could bring. A big basic capital "war chest" of this kind, perhaps approaching £1 billion and supporting much larger additional borrowings, could finance faster growth and allow speedy diversification into new areas through acquisitions and/or internally generated expansion. Good profits would be vital in view of the need to service the fresh capital with dividends. The ability of a public company to give management the incentive of "stock option" rights to buy shares on favourable terms was also noted.

At the same time the pressures the conversion process would place on senior management, and the risk of a failure to win members' support, were underlined, but thought manageable. The choice was described as "a once-in-a-lifetime decision" and the recommendation was that Abbey National should seek to convert to PLC status.

One senior executive director summed up the message as being: "You can stay mutual: it will see you lot out. You can just have a gently declining business over the next 30, 40 years ...."

Many had rather expected the consultants' report to point up the case for remaining mutual. The fact that this independent assessment came down so strongly the other way was very influential. John Fry remembers being totally persuaded by this report. He recalls: "From then on we had a united executive in favour of the PLC option," adding: "It's probably fair to say I was the last person to be converted."

Thus, early in 1986, the executive had formulated its own view in favour of the PLC option. Peter Birch then appointed John Fry as the head of corporate planning with the job of handling further preparatory work on the subject.

Before the end of January 1986 the society sent the Treasury its comments on the conversion clauses of the Building Societies Bill just published. As well as lobbying, with others, for less seemingly prohibitive voting thresholds, Abbey called for as much freedom as possible for a converting society to frame its own change-over scheme. On voting, it favoured members being balloted as a "single college" if borrowers were to have a say. There should be no minimum turnout and a two-thirds majority of those voting should suffice.

The broad thinking behind these and other detailed suggestions, it was explained, was that mutuality could become unsuitable for some societies, so conversion ought to be a real, available option. This paper, showing the extent of the executive's interest in conversion, was duly circulated to, and noted by, the board. But in spite of this, the government retained tough thresholds for conversion votes.

The Act became law in July 1986, with the majority of its provisions, giving the societies more operational elbow-room, due to come into force at the start of 1987. The conversions sections were only to take effect on January 1, 1988.

Peter Birch later summed up the executive's view that the wider powers conferred by the new Act could not give Abbey, as a building society, the scope it needed for the future.

"We said to ourselves: 'We are a fairly substantial organisation. We are constricted and constrained by the Building Societies Act. We don't have the freedom to compete.' We were somewhat critical of the new Act because it affected all building societies whether they had £100 million or £20 billion of assets, in exactly the same way.

"We felt we were of such a size that, with all the changes and deregulation taking place in the world, and the pace of change technologically, we needed in the future the freedom available through conversion. We required access to capital, and the 1986 Act did not give us access to share capital in the way we wanted, for instance, to make acquisitions."

The stage was now set for the next scene in which the executive formally asked Abbey National's varied and experienced board to back its aim of seeking to transform the society to company status.

The chairman had already warned his chief executive of his resolve to take an impartial approach during the process of consideration. "There were going to be no 'pro' noises from me. I thought that this was such a vital decision that for the chairman to start off being in favour or against would be quite wrong."

Later, Sir Campbell recalled that when Peter Birch had first disclosed that he favoured conversion, he himself was privately also "pretty convinced that we should become a PLC."

It is interesting that, in a preliminary note of July 1986 covering copies of earlier outside studies sent to directors as background reading, it was pointed out that, so far from being squeezed by competition as feared, Abbey's profits had continued to rise. One reason for this contradiction of earlier apprehensions was the prolonged credit boom which kept home-loans business buoyant for all players in Britain until the late-1980s; another was the effort made through cost-watching and otherwise to boost profitability.

Indeed, it is striking just how far building society profits in general were boosted from the early-1980s, despite the more competitive conditions. The main explanation is that, with previous curbs removed, pent-up mortgage demand was being satisfied at relatively higher rates than in the previous regulated era, with corresponding benefit to profit margins. It has been estimated that, of the building society movement's total reserves, representing accumulated profits, at the end of 1984, 48 per cent had been amassed since 1981.

So marked was the trend that Abbey National's own net profits in the three years to 1987 were more than doubled compared with the previous three years. The effect of this successful resistance to profit pressures was to make the arguments derived from fears that the market would run out of growth look perhaps less decisive. But Abbey National's executive held firmly to its longer-term conviction of the need for a future free from the limitations of building society status.

"Freedom to Compete" was to be the title of the executive's main submissions to the board, the first of which was submitted in November 1986.

Outlining the case for converting to PLC status it recalled the changed, more competitive climate in financial services with the banks' pursuit of more affluent mortgage borrowers and the emergence of fresh rivals, including foreign banks.

The unsuitability of mutual structure for a group as large as Abbey was argued and the risk of only restricted growth in this form if the mortgage market reached saturation was emphasised. By contrast, the removal of hampering curbs on activity and the access to equity capital to support business growth, possible acquisitions and stock option incentives to staff through conversion were underlined. The danger of these advantages being lost should a rival convert first was also mentioned.

A number of background points were included, one drawing attention to the increasingly broad range of competitors in financial services, including large stores groups. As to the conversion proposal, it was noted that the mere creation of the power to embrace the PLC option reflected government recognition that its choice could be right for some societies.

As to the status which would be abandoned, the paper, under the heading "The Myth of Mutuality," spotlighted the vast change that had taken place since the societies' origins in small, self-help groups of individuals. It suggested that a "mutual" constitution was somewhat outmoded for Britain's top building societies, which stood in the same size class as big banks and whose decision-making could not realistically be dictated by its membership.

The "romantic" view that mutual organisations are not profit maximisers was also criticised, as was the implication in it that a commercial company could not preserve the name and caring image that were an Abbey strength. The prolonged nature, complexities and demands on staff of the conversion process were recognised in the paper, but were not regarded as an obstacle to the change.

Finally, the board was told that the executive firmly believed the society must convert in due course if it was to achieve its corporate purpose. Authority was sought for the preparation of plans on the basis that, while the strategic direction would be endorsed, it would still be possible to pull back later.

The upshot of the discussion was that no decision to convert was made and it was agreed that there was a need to do more thinking on the crucial choice. The board requested papers further developing the arguments for and against conversion, and touching particularly on defences against the risks of takeover which a switch to public status could bring.

Sir Campbell Adamson later spoke of this initial formal focus by the directors on the subject. "We had a first preliminary discussion, a very cautious start. I don't recall, even at that meeting, anybody holding up their hands and saying: 'We don't want to talk about this, for God's sake. We're not going down this route.' I do recall quite a number of people saying: 'well, we would need to be persuaded.'"

The next major boardroom discussion of the topic would be in the following summer.

Meanwhile, Abbey's executives were given the go-ahead to continue planning without prejudice to the ultimate decision.

An important next step, taken early in 1987, was the appointment of a merchant bank as adviser. This was done through the customary process of a "beauty contest," or competitive interview. Teams from a short list of five leading City merchant bankers paraded before an interviewing panel consisting of Peter Birch, John Bayliss, John Fry, John Ellis and James Tyrrell.

Given the heavyweight entry, the choice was far from clear-cut in advance, but the selectors, operating a points-scoring system reminiscent of skating spectaculars, picked out Kleinwort Benson. One of the panel credits a sense of "chemistry, a feeling that this was going to work in terms of people" for the eventual choice of Kleinwort, which had in 1984 masterminded the major conversion and flotation exercise for British Telecom's privatisation.

David Clementi, the Kleinwort director who assumed general charge of the advisory work for Abbey National, later described the job as "A very prestigious transaction, a trend-setter, the first-of-a-type that every banker likes to do."

An early move by Kleinwort was to clarify that a building society was owned by its members in contrast with the recently-floated former Trustee Savings Banks which had no owners and whose situation had been cleared up by legislation. In June 1987, Timothy Lloyd, a leading QC, gave an opinion confirming that Abbey National's members did own the society.

This cleared the ground for the next stages of preparation and decision.

5

CLIVEDEN CLIMAX

THE BOARD which faced the biggest decision in Abbey National's history consisted of 12 men and two women. Only three of the 14, Peter Birch, John Bayliss and John Fry, were full-time directors.

The chairman, Sir Campbell Adamson, spent much time on the society's business but without having direct management responsibilities. Other non-executive directors, including the deputy chairman, Jeremy Rowe, performed tasks such as visiting branches in addition to their board duties but were only intermittently in the office. Most had other business or public roles.

Rowe, whose London Brick Company was taken over by Lord Hanson after a bid battle in 1984, had public responsibilities as chairman of the Occupational Pensions Board and of Peterborough Development Corporation.

Three of the directors were chairmen of Abbey's regional advisory boards. That in Scotland was headed by Sir Iain Tennant, a Scottish grandee and Knight of the Thistle who had extensive business interests. The Welsh Board was chaired by Hugh Rees, a chartered surveyor and a director of the Welsh Development Agency, and that in Northern Ireland by the businessman Sir Myles Humphreys.

Sir John Garlick, a former top Whitehall man, and the senior solicitor Sir Edward Singleton both had long experience in their fields, while Peter Davis was an accountant and finance chief of Sturge Holdings. Dame Jennifer Jenkins was known for both business and public roles, including her chairmanship of the National Trust.

One episode of board history is that Sara Morrison, the GEC businesswoman and former senior Conservative Party officer, was dislodged as a director in 1986 when a rival candidate defeated her by a small majority. The rival was Michael Heap, previously an Abbey branch manager, who won strong support from staff members wanting a former colleague on the board. There was nothing personal about the contest, though, and the next year Sara Morrison was re-appointed a director, Michael Heap retaining his place.

Although this meant a gap in her tenure, Sara Morrison was essentially part of the board which weighed the conversion issue between late-1986 and its decision in the spring of 1988 to take the PLC option. The society's secretary, John Ellis, increased the numbers in the crucial group who made the final decision on conversion to 15.

It was not to be expected that such a varied body would quickly find itself of one mind on the complex question facing them. Attachment to the familiar mutual structure was considerable, while the untried obstacle course towards conversion was terrain which could prove daunting and costly. Nor did the case for a change seem at once convincing to all, as the initial discussion in November 1986 had shown. The board decided to consider the issue in stages and earmarked certain special "strategic" board meetings to review it.

One of the group's most active outside directors recaptures some of the thinking shared by himself and certain colleagues from around the mid-1980s into 1987. "The non-executive members of the board tended at this stage to be rather sceptical about going PLC, for two reasons. First of all, we hadn't given much thought to doing the sorts of things such a change would facilitate. This was because we hadn't, until late-1986, had Big Bang [the stock market shakeup involving new diversification for the large banks], and the great cross-fertilisation of activities everybody then engaged in. So the idea of doing business in Europe or buying a chain of estate agents, which everybody was subsequently going to be doing, hadn't really formed part of our culture at Abbey National.

"The second factor was some uncertainty whether, despite top level outside recruitment, the management - and we were only a few years out from the cosy cartel world - would be up to coping with the rough and tumble of PLC life.

"We touched on the conversion subject briefly from time to time, and there was a strong theme in those early days of the executives saying that we couldn't compete on a level playing-field with other financial institutions if we stayed mutual; for example we could not get access to funding on the best terms. Yet others argued that we had done very well and maintained our position as a mutual.

"The non-executive board members took the line: 'We're not prepared to drift into going PLC because it's got some good points. We want a hard look taken at the two alternative scenarios - our future as a mutual and our future as a PLC.'"

The consultants' report which had favoured conversion afforded one response to this requirement. The next was the pair of papers giving the case for and against conversion, which the board had requested at the end of 1986.

Sara Morrison, industrialist, ex-politician and Abbey's first woman director who was part of the team which first weighed the conversion issue.

These papers, together with a covering one by Peter Birch presenting the executive's strong recommendation of continued preparation for the PLC option, were considered by directors at a strategic board meeting in June 1987.

A new "Freedom to Compete" paper spelled out in fresh detail the case for switching status, arguing that there was a strong need to diversify.

First, there was the increased risk of being in a "one product" home loans business when the mortgage market was maturing. Then there were the desirability of branching out into related businesses to support or defend the "core" mortgage side and the case for moving into rewarding new sectors, hitherto the province of rival financial groups. Also, research had shown that Abbey's customers would welcome, and respond to, their group supplying a wide range of financial services.

The need for more capital both to support new activities and to retain a good mortgage market share was emphasised. Although there were various sources of this, none had the advantages of equity shares that could be used to raise cash or to finance acquisitions. It would be open to a converted Abbey National to make such share issues.

Commercial status would also permit the group to expand overseas without the restrictions imposed on building societies and so provide scope for its development as a world player.

In short, the paper summed up the limitations which continued building society status threatened to impose on the group's growth. It also stressed the inadequate scope Abbey would have with its existing status, even if societies' powers were widened afresh under the Act. By contrast, the access to major new capital which PLC status would give could open for the group great future opportunities, including developments abroad, allowing it to become a world player. Freedom from vexatiously close regulation was noted as another virtue of corporate structure.

At the same time the accompanying paper setting out the other side of the case provided a telling defence of the existing structure. Entitled "The Mutualist Viewpoint," it argued that none of the new Act's limits would prevent Abbey from fulfilling the ambitious five-year development programme it had adopted in 1986. Given that the society would soon be able to raise a new form of "subordinated" capital, access to equity was really unnecessary. Moreover, conversion to company status could, the paper suggested, lose Abbey its image as a friendly and caring institution.

The chief executive's paper, coming down firmly in favour of conversion, stressed how fitted Abbey National was to establish itself as a leader in the personal banking sector. In PLC form, the group would have much better access to wholesale funds and equity capital, while being freed to compete unfettered by the Building Societies Act.

It was not believed that any difficulties of the conversion process (expected to cost, at most, £75 million) were insuperable. "The Society," directors were reminded, "has a reputation for leading change, it is commercially driven, it is adaptable, it is tightly managed and it is aware of what is happening in the competitive financial services market place."

At this mid-1987 board meeting, the debate flowed to and fro. Again no decision was reached. The main conclusions were, first, that the group's "corporate purpose" should be reviewed as a logical prelude to the structure decision. More work should also be done on the priorities for diversification and research conducted on the likely membership and staff reaction to a conversion decision. The future as it would be, should the society stay mutual, was also to be explored further.

A senior Abbey insider remarks about this stage: "The general tenor of meetings was that a lot of directors were instinctively in favour of mutuality and feared the management were trying to tow the board along, to some extent to steamroller the whole idea of conversion through."

The arrival of November and the next board session on conversion marked a significant fresh step towards a conclusion. Various doubts persisted but a year had now passed since the first formal discussion and in some minds at least, the idea was hardening that the time for decision was approaching.

At least one director felt that a trend towards conversion was under way which would be difficult to halt. "What I think was happening was that the board was being edged along, rightly in a way, to confront this absolutely major issue," he said.

Further papers were considered, leading the board to adopt a revised corporate purpose for the group, namely "Excellence and value in meeting personal financial needs."

Important shifts in the world outside provided a significant backdrop to the directors' discussion on conversion. The banks had in 1987 resumed their attack on the mortgage market and captured so much new business that the societies' total market share dropped in the year to an unprecedently low 52 per cent. This further fuelled Abbey's fears about the future of its traditional business.

The stock market boom had also exerted a counter-pull on personal funds, forcing societies to compete harder for individual savings and causing them even more to covet access to cheaper wholesale money. These factors tended to support the case for conversion even though funds had been reflowing to the safety-first haven of the societies in the weeks since the "Black Monday" share crash in October.

Another recent development lending extra urgency to the late-1987 discussion was that other building societies, including the largest, the Halifax, and the big Nationwide Anglia and the Woolwich, were also looking at the conversion option. The danger that a rival society might move a step ahead and reap the gains foreseen for the first society to gain bank status was a goad towards reaching an early decision.

Among points hammered home by Peter Birch to the November meeting in a plea for the conversion option were that Abbey

National, as an operation in a one-product, mature business, needed to diversify at substantial expense and that its requirement to raise funds competitively had never been greater. As to the powers under the 1986 Act, these were too hampering for the group's needs; they were, he said, "a corset."

One director remembers it once more being a strong theme of the executive's case that Abbey just did not enjoy a level-playing field with other financial institutions.

At this board meeting Sir Iain Tennant told his fellow directors that the Scottish advisory board had discussed conversion and favoured it. Report has it that he added: "We wonder why the hell you don't just get on with it."

The director who had earlier been among those pressing for a presentation of both sides of the case recalls that by late-1987 events had set a new context for decision. For one thing, the new wave of bank incursion into the mortgage market was important: "The banks had demonstrated that they could, if they set their minds to it, take over a majority of our business in terms of new lending."

Then, Big Bang had made it much clearer that other financial bodies were diversifying, Lloyds Bank's move into estate agency being significant here. The board had also grown more convinced of Abbey top management having the needed financial sophistication to play in a wider field.

It was now arranged that the board should convene for a special one-and-a-half-day strategic conference about the conversion issue on January 22-23, 1988 at Cliveden House. This is the celebrated Buckinghamshire mansion, which was once the home of members of the Astor family and is now both a National Trust property and a hotel.

To ensure that the board had all necessary reading matter for this summit, a sub-group of four directors was chosen to vet the choice of papers to be provided. Its members were Jeremy Rowe, the deputy chairman, Sir John Garlick, Sara Morrison and Peter Davis. More than one of the foursome recall that the first list seemed "too one-sided" in favour of conversion, so changes were introduced.

A bulky tome of documents, with an introductory review and 19 appendices, was assembled for the Cliveden conclave. It included material on "Mutuality" and "The PLC Option," along with detailed papers on marketing, technology, housing, personnel and other issues, including Abbey National's corporate philosophy.

Two key subjects were on the agenda: the functions that

should make up the group's range of activities and the best structural form - mutual or PLC - for achieving them. It was obviously logical to deal with the first topic before tackling the second.

The directors assembled in the big house overlooking the Thames on the cold Friday lunchtime of January 22, each with the weighty dossier. To allow ample time for discussing the big issues, the chairman had asked board members to arrive having read the papers, which would not be taken individually but treated as background.

At the first session there was an address by an invited academic contributor, Professor Tadeusz Rybczynski, a former economic adviser to Lazards, the City merchant bank of which Sir Campbell Adamson had long been a director. This extensive talk ranged over the globalisation, modernisation and de-regulation of the world money industry which had greatly widened the role and composition of financial institutions in a kind of restructuring, or "perestroika."

Answering questions, the professor voiced the view that the present building society legislation would not survive and that "mutuality" among major institutions would not endure. This opinion made a substantial impact.

The board then proceeded to focus on the group's future range of business activities. There was general support for the creation of an estate agency chain. However, the directors did not want Abbey, whatever its corporate structure, to become a large-scale commercial lender like the big banks, still less a provider of international and Third World finance. At the other end of the spectrum, peripheral retail activities such as running ice-cream parlours were ruled out.

In short, the board's wish was to emphasise the existing core business and to add suitably to it, though without replicating the business span of the main banks. It was agreed that the exact future range of financial services needed more thought, as did overseas expansion, but that meanwhile the branch network - the link with the millions of valued clients - should be improved. Not until the next day, Saturday, was the gathering to turn to the "mutual or PLC" question. The issue would simmer in people's minds as the conference broke off for dinner and a night's rest in the luxurious venue.

Cliveden is an impressive pile of a building, in mellow country and with a long history as a private house hosting social-political gatherings. Two board members, Sir Iain Tennant and Sara Morrison, remembered visiting there in earlier days, the latter as a young girl with her horses. Dame Jennifer Jenkins had a special connection with the property, owned as it is by the National Trust; as the Trust's chairman, she toured the grounds in a chilly break between sessions to view trees damaged in the hurricane three months before.

For its business sessions the board met in slightly cramped conditions in the Mountbatten Room, the best conference room then available. They were seated round a long thin mahogany table, from the top of which Sir Campbell presided and which sometimes barely held the large bundles of paper with which the directors had been issued.

Dinner on Friday evening proved a convivial meal. So special was the occasion that Peter Davis, the City man who was later to become deputy chairman, was persuaded to break his annual vow of abstention from alcohol in January and try the excellent wine.

A sketch of Cliveden House, the Buckinghamshire mansion where, in January 1988, Abbey's directors crystallised their views on the conversion option.

As to the whole atmosphere of this historic rendezvous, John Ellis, the company secretary, later reflected on the significance of the setting: "It was really the ideal location for that kind of conference. It is the only stately home that is also a hotel - very picturesque, in lovely scenery and with great paintings on the walls. I think it helped to bring home the awesomeness of the momentous decision that was to be made. It is quite a grand place. And we felt that it was the right sort of context and scene for the nature of the occasion."

Throughout the two days, in formal sessions and informal breaks, the thoughts of all would centre on the one key decision - conversion - which would decide Abbey National's future.

A full-time director remembers of the conference: "It was

remarkably relaxed and everybody could say what they wanted. As usual Campbell chaired in a way that was extremely impartial and extremely effective."

There is no doubt that some directors, almost certainly a minority, went to Cliveden still undecided in their own minds on the crucial conversion issue. There are references in recollections to waverers and to uncertainties of various kinds. "I think there was a genuine arrival at Cliveden without fixed conclusive views," says one director. And "conversion certainly was not at all a foregone conclusion," remembers another, who is conscious of having arrived at Cliveden as one of perhaps four doubters.

A different view, however, is that by this time - January 1988 - opinion had already hardened significantly towards a pro-PLC position. "There were several board members who were undecided, but they weren't a strong lobby at all," one recalls. There are also signs that there was a swing of feeling during the conference, particularly after Professor Rybczynski's views on the poor long-term prospects for mutuality.

Sir Campbell later remembered of Professor Rybczynski: "He painted a worldwide picture of how he thought banking and financial services would look in a few years. He got us worried about the future. I've sometimes wondered since whether, if I hadn't asked him, we'd have come out quite as clearly as we did at the end."

Some directors were convinced by particular arguments. For instance, one with much attachment to the mutual tradition acknowledges: "I was bowled middle-stump on the argument of capital adequacy and our being able as a PLC to raise money in sufficient quantities."

Another recalls: "You might say we were coming round to what the executive had said 18 months earlier. I would prefer to put it that circumstances were changing in a way that made the judgment a couple of years later the right one, while the judgment a couple of years earlier [not then to give the go-ahead] might also have been the right one at the time. Two years on, the risks were less and the benefits more important, because the downside of not doing it became more risky."

In the course of the Cliveden meeting directors heard that the Halifax, the only society larger than Abbey National, were appointing N. M. Rothschild, the merchant bank, to advise it on matters to do with conversion. This news caused a frisson and perhaps provided yet more impetus towards reaching a decision.

As the directors formally faced up to the critical issue on Saturday, the familiar arguments were rehearsed. It was again urged that the group needed the operational flexibility and access to capital which the Act, at its fullest stretch, could not allow and which only PLC status could provide. Against this the claim was heard that the society could build on its past success in unaltered form, the more so since societies' powers might soon be considerably widened.

Eventually the chairman said he sensed the board was on the whole inclined towards the conversion option. Sir Campbell then proceeded to ask for the view of each director on whether or not to convert.

It would perhaps have been surprising, if within a varied board on such a long-debated crucial issue, there had not been one dissentient from the emerging majority view.

The deputy chairman, Jeremy Rowe, was unpersuaded of the need for conversion, preferring that Abbey should stay focused on housing finance rather than take the course of transforming, as he saw it, into a retail bank. Rowe naturally made his view plain to his colleagues, as he had before. But by now he was isolated in a board with an overwhelmingly pro-PLC stance.

Sir Campbell later spoke of how he gathered up opinions and his reaction to the result. "I was immensely surprised when, at the end of Cliveden, we went round the table. Every single person said they thought we should go PLC except Jeremy Rowe. Jeremy - he's quite courageous if he doesn't agree with the mob - made a reasonably impassioned speech as to why we shouldn't do this and why we shouldn't do it now. So I had 14-to-one."

The chairman, who had thus far taken care to keep his own view in the background - though most directors by then reckoned him in favour - next confirmed that he also was of the majority view backing conversion.

Rather than endorse the decision then and there he insisted, however, that there should be an interval for more thought before the final choice two months ahead at the board meeting in March. But nobody now doubted that the decision had essentially been made.

A discussion next took place on the timing of conversion. Up to this point, it had seemed likely that the move, if finally approved, could be some way off, perhaps in the winter of 1989-1990, or later, though it could be earlier.

An important point on this aspect was now stressed. This was that, because the Labour Party had opposed the conversion provisions of the Act, a change of government in the early-1990s could remove the PLC opportunity, which should thus be seized without too much delay. This argument commanded wide support.

The virtual consensus at Cliveden for taking Abbey National into the company sector, despite considerable arguments both ways, was a triumph for the executive management with its convinced and unanimous stance in favour of that policy.

One illuminating later comment from a once-doubting director among the majority touched on the inappropriateness of blocking such a determined management. "It would have been too onerous a decision to persuade the executive to stick with building society status and perhaps de-motivate them when they were so committed." One of the other supporting non-executives described the conclusion as "an instinctive one, a gut-feeling."

Another board member notes: "I think it's fair to say that, during Cliveden, quite a lot of people adjusted their ideas." One more director remembers having come to a sense during the sessions that the days of building societies might anyway be numbered, a factor making the PLC action more eligible.

The role of Sir Campbell's own view in the decision was also very important, despite the impartiality with which he presided over the long decision-making. A businessman himself, he had long privately favoured a change to PLC status. A top executive, asked afterwards whether the board could, practically speaking, have overturned the executive's view, replied: "The key figure is Campbell, as chairman. If he had set his face against conversion, the non-executives would have lined up behind him."

The process by which Abbey worked its way towards its choice is a vivid illustration of how a major institution with a largely non-executive board settled policy on a crucial, yet debatable question. This can perhaps be seen as an instance of the kind of situation where there is a strong management sense in favour of a course of action, with a resolve to follow it, notwithstanding that the case could be argued either way. The outcome in this case shows how an executive, marked by clear vision and determination, and enjoying the chairman's sympathy and the directors' confidence, had its plan endorsed by a board, some of whose members had earlier felt considerable hesitation.

Peter Birch later, after the tough process of conversion had been successfully completed, summed up what had been the executive's confident conception. "We believed we could cope very well as a public company and that we would be in a better position to look after customer needs and be a good service company in that form. We felt it was right for the business. It was a very open and shut case so far as we were concerned."

Jeremy Rowe, who found himself in the unenviable position of odd-man-out, said later: "The argument that we would have to convert to compete with the banks to my mind didn't really stand up. Nor did I feel that there was a solid enough case in relation to raising new capital. Although I was not necessarily opposed to conversion for all time, I believed the building societies would be able to raise the capital needed without conversion, as such groups as the Halifax have shown. I do believe that, as a non-executive, you should at the end of the day make your own opinion clear." It was an assertion of view that would raise questions within his own mind about the role of the non-executive director, in particular whether to stand to his beliefs even to the point of resigning or whether to concede to his colleagues, thus providing the board with the unanimous recommendation to the membership that was felt important in getting conversion through.

It was not quite goodbye to Cliveden for all the participants when, in the early evening of Saturday, the party dispersed after their two-day get-together. As it happened, both Sir Campbell and Peter Davis had arranged, unknown to each other, to be joined by their wives for a further day's stay over in the Cliveden atmosphere at their own expense.

So Campbell and Mimi Adamson and Peter and Vanessa Davis dined in a foursome that evening, perhaps enjoying chatting about the two days' events. They were not the only ones to have been sufficiently taken with the venue to revisit it off-duty. As both families were packing their cars for departure, they met two other senior Abbey National couples, John and Maureen Bayliss and John and Diana Fry, arriving for Sunday lunch together at the house.

As intended, the February board meeting did not attempt a final decision. Instead, directors reviewed matters that would arise assuming a go-ahead was given, including certain tax questions.

The board also considered a recent government decision that the powers of building societies, which were by then able to raise 40 per cent of their funds on the wholesale markets, were to be further widened. The changes would, among other things, allow societies to provide more banking services, give personal loans up to £10,000 and gradually increase to 25 per cent the proportion of their business to other than first-mortgage lending.

But this prompted no policy re-appraisal. Since the changes would not enable the group to raise equity capital or deploy its assets as flexibly as if it were a bank, it was felt they could not give what Abbey needed.

David Clementi, a veteran of the Telecom flotation. In general charge of the work for merchant bank advisers Kleinwort Benson, he helped draw up Abbey's conversion scheme and was part of the team who fixed the flotation price tag of 130p.

The tax question was important since, unless special arrangements were made, the conversion process threatened to attract heavy and unintended tax changes. Abbey National had kept in touch with the government, which was generally friendly towards its PLC aspirations, while taking no general policy stance for or against conversion. Both it and the Building Societies Association had explained the tax difficulty to the Treasury, in particular to Peter Lilley, then Economic Secretary.

The result was that, in his Budget, the Chancellor, Nigel Lawson, announced special reliefs; having willed the possibility of conversion, the government was ready to remove unplanned obstacles to it. These measures, which were added to during the Finance Bill's passage, were announced a week before Abbey's decisive board meeting on March 22.

At that meeting, Sir Campbell asked his fellow-directors if they had had second thoughts on conversion. Nobody had but Jeremy Rowe took this last chance to repeat his own reservations. At the same time, he said he appreciated the importance of a unanimous decision. He had too much respect for his colleagues to wish to dissent from an otherwise agreed conclusion so, if the PLC option was to be taken, he would loyally support it.

In a formal vote a decision to recommend to members that the society should convert into a PLC was then taken unanimously. Following this, the board closed ranks for the future, whatever uncertainties had been felt before.

Given the sharp division between his views and his colleagues', the question had arisen of Jeremy Rowe's possible resignation. However, it was arranged that he should remain, although Peter Davis was appointed as a second deputy chairman. In the event Jeremy Rowe's earlier opposition never came to light and he continued as a deputy chairman and director until October 1989. By then, three months after conversion, the dust had settled and he was able to retire quietly from the board after 13 years' service.

The conversion project was announced the next day when Sir Campbell said that the changeover would provide "the freedom we need to compete on the same basis as our major competitors." No timetable for the move was given.

News that Abbey planned to be the first building society to take the plunge into the commercial arena at once captured top TV, radio and Press billing.

Sir Campbell told BBC TV's "Newsnight" programme: "We intend to become a major force in the High Street. But we do not intend, nor want, to be a bank as such. We want to be the same old Abbey National as we've always been, with people wanting to go in the doors and feeling happy about it."

The query "whether?" had been answered: the question of "how?" next loomed.

Sir Iain Tennant, who joined the board in 1981. His Scottish advisory board wondered "why the hell you (his board colleagues) don't get on with conversion."

John Ellis, Abbey's company secretary since 1979 and the "guardian" of procedures and culture. He was an early enthusiast of conversion.

6

DESIGNING THE SCHEME

ONCE Abbey National's directors had opted in March 1988 to seek the society's transformation into a public company, the management faced a thousand-and-one follow-up tasks.

The work on this first-ever conversion was split up and overseen by a number of "task forces," so called to reflect the theme of action, rather than the idea which the word "committee" evokes. Most of the group's top people were involved, several chairing a task force.

Below these directing bodies, which met at intervals, numerous staff laboured, often more than full-time, in close concert with the advisers, notably the City solicitors Slaughter & May, the merchant bank Kleinwort Benson and the accountants Deloitte. These and other advisers were also represented on the task forces.

At the apex was the overseeing executive task force, chaired by Peter Birch as chief executive, with a remit to "arbitrate and resolve key issues." The structure task force, entrusted with devising the conversion scheme, was headed by John Fry, the group services director who was assigned to work full-time at board level on the project.

It was also a central aim that conversion work should not distract the management from its principal job of running and developing the business. The fact that 1988 and 1989 saw good profits growth as well as expansion in insurance, estate agency, pension and other new services shows that this objective was met.

There were to be several landmarks in the conversion procedure. Five million-plus members eligible to decide would receive a detailed description of the conversion scheme, on the basis of which they would be asked to vote for or against it, mainly through proxy

Designing the scheme

forms. If they said "Yes," the scheme would next need the seal of approval from the Building Societies Commission watchdog.

After that would come the vital stage of an offer of new shares to bring in the large fresh capital required. When that operation had been carried out, the society's change-over would be completed with the handover of its business to its PLC successor, whose shares would at once be launched on the Stock Exchange.

Not much could be done before a timetable was constructed and this in turn depended on when the essential share sale could be made. The sum to be raised was so large - around £1 billion, perhaps more - that the issue had to be scheduled well away from big privatisation cash calls like those for Water and Electricity. By the early summer of 1988, a "slot" for Abbey's issue, in May - June 1989, had been pencilled in with the Bank of England's agreement. Some months earlier, preliminary thinking had been that the date might be up to six months later.

The timing meant that the special general meeting to reveal the verdict from the massive ballot would be in April 1989. The "transfer document" presenting the scheme would have to be distributed with voting forms to more than five million recipients some weeks before that. Drafting of this crucial communication, again a first of its kind, required an Everest of effort, as did logistical preparations for the printing and despatch of this, and much other, paperwork.

The rest of the programme took shape accordingly. First outlined by Kleinwort in August 1988, it thereafter changed little. However, the "road show" programme of members' meetings which Sir Campbell Adamson and Peter Birch held round the country to explain the scheme was postponed from late-autumn 1988 to January-February 1989.

The whole timetable proved extremely tight given all there was to be done. The Building Societies Commission, which had statutory responsibilities and closely monitored all developments, later complained of being rushed. But the need to avoid a clash with privatisations dictated the hectic schedule, with certain consequential strains and stresses. The alternative of a long wait, perhaps well into 1991 after Electricity's privatisation, could not have been acceptable to Abbey National once its pro-PLC stance had been taken.

At the heart of the whole process was the conversion scheme itself, framed under the law but shaped, too, by many deliberate choices. The Act set a framework requiring the transfer of the society's business at the moment of transformation on "Vesting Day" to a specially-created company, Abbey National PLC. In effect "savings" would then become "deposits" in the latter, which would have banking status and to which borrowers would in future owe their loans.

Although this formal hand-over of business was what conversion as such was all about, there had never been any doubt that it would need to be coupled with a big cash-raising operation. This would involve the sale of shares for cash to raise the major sum of capital which the group, in its new bank-style form, would need in order to satisfy exacting Bank of England requirements. Equally certainly, the new PLC's share capital, distributed among millions of new holders, would be quoted and traded on the stock market through a "flotation."

A key matter was who would have the shares representing ownership of Abbey National PLC, which was taking over the existing business worth £1.42 billion in accumulated reserves.

There were two main possibilities. Shares reflecting the value of the society could be distributed free to its existing members, either equally or in some other pattern, with cash being raised against the issue of further shares. Alternatively, all shares of the new Abbey National PLC could be put up for sale to bring in the amount wanted. This offer could be to Abbey members only, to the public at large, or to the latter, but with preferential allocation to Abbey applicants.

The second approach, in this last form, had been the one followed when TSB Group was floated in 1986. It was possible to use a mixture of the two methods and variations on them.

John Fry set about devising the scheme, working closely with David Clementi, Lesley Watts, and John Williams of Kleinwort, and Slaughter's Nick Wilson and Tim Clark. Their job was bedevilled by the obscurity of the Act's conversion sections, which seemed to envisage a TSB-type approach but could accommodate other methods.

Records show that as early as December 1987 Kleinwort sketched the idea of a free share distribution to members, giving them the net worth of the society as it stood just before conversion. But by the time of the board's decision in March 1988 to seek a switch to PLC status, thinking had rather swung - in tune with the Act - towards a TSB-type scheme of all shares being for sale.

However, the latter kind of scheme had marked drawbacks. For one thing, it would have meant that members would have to put

Designing the scheme

up money to buy shares if they were to participate in the rewards of conversion. This would scarcely be fair or popular given that, legally, a building society was owned by its members.

Another major problem with a cash-only share issue was that it would mean a big windfall profit, representing the existing worth of the transferred business to those - perhaps including non-members - who bought shares. The arithmetic of the matter was such that this profit could only be "diluted" by raising more money than was needed against an unsuitably large issue of new shares.

This type of objection, which reflected criticism heard in the TSB case, weighed heavily against a scheme of this kind. More importantly, the method was judged not sufficiently generous to recognise members' rights and uncertain to win their support.

Various schemes involving free shares, all combined with a cash issue, were then reviewed between April and June 1988. One canvassed for a while would have involved free shares being allotted to members in stages over time and held in a trust until distribution. The aim was to fend off any swamping of the market should millions of members seek to cash in by selling all at once. Again, this was ultimately thought to give inadequate encouragement and recognition to members.

One problem facing the planners over the cash issue was that, under the Act, if Abbey members got priority in putting in for shares over other subscribers, this privilege could only be accorded to those of two years' standing. At the time, moreover, the society's computer systems were unable to pick out savers of this standing. In any event, it seemed unfair and would be unpopular to deny favourable share-buying to newer members.

By June, the planners came up with the outline of the scheme finally adopted. A fixed number of free shares (later set at 100) would be issued to all qualifying members, this in effect allocating to them the society's worth at conversion. In addition, there would be a cash offer of extra shares which, it was eventually decided, would be to members only. The sum to be raised, whether £1 billion, £1.5 billion or even more, was left to be finalised later.

Nick Wilson of Slaughters, who returned in July after a three month sabbatical which took him to the Great Wall of China, recalls how wonderfully the scheme had evolved in his absence, when his colleague Tim Clark had "borne the heat and burden of the day."

The scheme, which was approved in principle by the board in June, was filled out with a good deal of further detail by the autumn.

For instance, it was only then settled that there should be no deferment in the issue of the free shares and that they should all be distributed by the moment the shares were first traded.

A further decision was that, when it came to the cash issue, all applicants would be guaranteed a minimum allocation, once more encouraging a wide and fairly equal share spread.

Many important details of the scheme flowed from deliberate choices by Abbey. Free shares, and the entitlement to buy extra ones, should, it was decided, go to all members entitled to vote, in essence all the members except minors (children under 18) and savers with less than £100. This meant borrowers as well as savers being included, with double entitlements for people who were both savers and borrowers.

Nicholas Wilson of Slaughter & May, a member of Abbey's team of legal advisers who worked at the heart of the conversion scheme. It was a job bedevilled by the obscurity of the Building Societies Act 1986.

The law and the society's standard rules settled which members had the vote: Abbey decided that these should be broadly the recipients of the benefits of conversion. The excluded categories of minors and small savers were, as the law required, compensated with a cash payment proportionate to their holdings. Later legal complications also disqualified certain overseas members from receiving share benefits.

John Fry, who guided the scheme's creation, said afterwards: "We thought the fairest way would be to say: 'Mutuality is all about one member, one vote. That means one member, one tranche of free shares.' The scheme reflected members' ownership of the society in a tangible way."

Naturally this policy, by widely extending the benefits of

conversion, was an incentive - unkind critics called it a bribe - to vote for the conversion plan.

A further choice, made on the same "mutual" principle, was to give a fixed all-round allocation of free shares rather than one related to the size of a member's savings. The possibility of gearing the free share issue to the scale of savings was thought about, but this would have been complicated and could have been hard on those who had lately withdrawn holdings. It was rejected as out of step with the basic "one vote, one allocation" principle.

In a further choice, it was decided to give the share entitlements to staff, not all of whom were necessarily members.

The essential linkage of share entitlements to those with voting rights involved some unpopular consequences. It had the effect of excluding second and any later holders in joint accounts, mostly wives. Worse, it denied shares to the widow of a member who, had he lived, would have qualified. These problems mostly became clear after the scheme had taken a set shape.

Abbey obviously felt its democratic "one vote, one entitlement" principle (though this was slightly qualified by including staff) afforded a clear and defensible basis for the scheme, whereas any other would have raised a host of new problems. Nonetheless, one lesson from Abbey's experience is that the exact ambit of entitlement may need fresh consideration in any future conversion. Whether or not any heed should be taken of size of savings in fixing entitlements could be another point for debate.

The mechanics of conversion involved the creation of the Abbey National PLC and its later reshaping into the right form to take over from the building society in accordance with a detailed transfer agreement between the two under the Act.

The new company was set up on September 12 1988 with £50,000 of capital. Its first directors were John Ellis, general manager and secretary of the society, who held 49,999 shares on the society's behalf; Norman Wilkes, assistant secretary, who held one share; and Ian Treacy, deputy secretary. All three resigned at a special meeting on February 28, 1989 and were succeeded by a board made up of exactly the people who were the society's directors.

At the same time Abbey National PLC's capital was revamped, the £50,000 being expanded to £56 million in 10p shares. This was to allow 100 free shares (560 million altogether) to be handed round to each of the estimated 5.6 million qualified recipients. Four months later, 750 million extra shares were issued under the flotation, so that

Abbey National PLC made its stock market debut with £131 million of share capital in 1.31 billion 10p shares. (The first quoted share price of 161p thus gave the newly listed group a market value of more than £2 billion).

The transfer agreement was signed on March 1, 1989, immediately after the capital revamping and shortly before the despatch of the detailed transfer document explaining the scheme to members and asking them to vote on it.

Tim Clark, an Abbey's legal adviser with Slaughter & May who was at the heart of the legal marathon to covert to PLC status.

Some debate preceded the original naming of the new company. Because the group planned, in its fresh incarnation, to stick to the broad field of personal financial services, eschewing commercial and international lending, it did not want to call itself Abbey National Bank.

But was there a middle-way term, parallel, say, to "hatchback" in motor parlance, between "saloon" and "estate car?" The search for the right "hatchback" word - might it be "trust" or "savings company?" - proved fruitless and the simple, familiar style "Abbey National" was adopted.

Although Abbey's ground-breaking conversion scheme was not of the "TSB" type that might have been expected on a first study of the Act, the society had been assured of its legality by its advisers, including Timothy Lloyd, QC, who was repeatedly consulted. The society also took the precaution of satisfying itself that the government did not expect the "TSB" model to be slavishly followed and would be content if the design complied with the law.

The agreement, between Abbey National Building Society and

Designing the scheme

Abbey National PLC, provided in detail for the business of the former to pass to the latter on "Vesting Day" (ultimately July 12, 1989), and for numerous associated arrangements. In particular, the hand-over was to be conditional on the new PLC's shares obtaining a Stock Exchange listing, on the granting to it of a Bank of England licence (authorisation) and on the execution of a trust deed securing the "priority liquidation distribution." The latter was the statutory arrangement giving converted PLC's savers, who continued as depositors, certain rights in the improbable event of the new company's being wound up.

Further refinements to the plan were added as the autumn of 1988 progressed. There was much worry that large savers could "disenfranchise" themselves after qualifying day (to be set at December 31, 1988) by pulling out their savings thereby, instead, becoming entitled to a percentage cash payment which could be worth more than free shares on their end-1988 savings. To fend off this risk, the society insisted that all accounts must remain open, even with a minimal 1p, from qualifying day to Vesting Day (July 12).

There were contingency plans under which the qualifying day might have been fixed earlier than the end of December 1988 if speculative inflows had developed. But this proved unnecessary. Not even following a story in the Evening Standard on December 12, 1988, correctly guessing that there would be free shares, was there any unusual savings intake.

The next stage would be the public unveiling, early in the New Year, of the outline of the conversion scheme and the timetable under which five million members would be asked to give their "Yea" or "Nay" verdict to the plan. But matters were not going to proceed smoothly. There was still a joker in the pack.

7

A COURT CLIFFHANGER

AGAINST the festive backdrop of Christmas, work progressed on the public announcement of the conversion scheme. Without warning, a legal obstacle suddenly appeared.

It was raised by the societies' regulator, the Building Societies Commission which, under the Act, had to approve the "statutory" parts of the coming transfer document and also later confirm the conversion if members voted for it. This meant that the Commission needed to be satisfied that the different stages of the process had been properly conducted. As regulator, it also asserted, evidently on legal advice, that a society had a fiduciary duty to put both sides of the case in submitting to members a plan to gain PLC status.

Chairing the Commission, and thus destined for a significant part in Abbey National's conversion saga, was Michael Bridgeman, a former senior Whitehall official in his mid-fifties with a spare-time passion for railways. Deeply knowledgeable about building societies from his early days in the Treasury, he had left that Department to head the Registry of Friendly Societies, which took its modern form as the Building Societies Commission from 1986. With a reputation for successfully watching over his sector and for meticulous attention to his responsibilities, Bridgeman has been known to be referred to by his charges as "the schoolmaster."

In a speech in May 1988 to the Building Societies Association's annual conference, he emphasised: "It is important that a [society's] board explains to the membership the potential consequences of conversion, favourable and unfavourable, as objectively as possible." The same point was made in the Commission's 1988 report. It was against this background of law and concerned interest that Abbey's planners took pains to keep the Commission in the closest touch throughout with its preparations.

From the start of planning, proposals were shown in confidence to the Commission, usually to a full-time Commissioner, Terry Mathews, a 53-year old former Treasury man. The outline of the free shares scheme was imparted in June 1988. As when other plans were shown to it, the Commission's response was that the particulars were noted. The time for formal consents would come later.

Over a number of months there was no sign of the Commission raising anything in the nature of a yellow card, still less a red card, of objection to what was shown to it. Until, that is, in December when a problem arose which threatened to strike at the very heart of the project.

The Commission had received Counsel's opinion that the underwriting arrangements - by which City bodies would agree to buy up any cash-offer shares not wanted by Abbey's members - fell foul of the Act's preferential rights provision. Abbey's own Counsel had, by contrast, viewed the plans as in line with the law.

It was a few days before Christmas that the Commission proposed a "friendly" legal case to obtain the Court's ruling on the issue and indeed on other key aspects of the scheme. However, as this process might take two months to complete in the normal course, the proposal threatened to wreck Abbey's whole timetable. With such a delay, the elaborate countdown to the key vote in April, the cash offer in June and conversion in July could not proceed on schedule.

From the moment this difficulty surfaced, a crisis-ridden three and a half weeks began for John Fry. With Slaughter's Nick Wilson, he first sought to test out alternative underwriting arrangements with Michael Bridgeman but, report has it, the Commission's chief declined to pronounce on "multiple-choice questions."

It was decided that John Fry should seek an emergency vacation Court hearing. Abbey agreed to the Commission's suggestion that the further aspects the case should cover would be the free share issue and the limits of the cash distribution for non-voting members.

Preparations sped forward and Slaughter's litigation expert, Tom Nelson, who happened to live near John Fry in Hertfordshire, called at the latter's home with drafts more than once during the 1988 Christmas break.

Highly sensitive to the remotest problems, Abbey worried lest any Judge who heard its case could be thought prejudiced were he or she a saver or borrower with the society. Accordingly, it ran the names of all the Chancery Court Judges through its computer to see if any was an Abbey member. None was. "A case for a mailshot to the Chancery Bench," quipped one insider.

As it happened, the chief Chancery Judge, the Vice-Chancellor, Sir Nicholas Browne-Wilkinson, was the Vacation Judge on duty from Tuesday, January 3, 1989.

John Fry, still in written dialogue with Michael Bridgeman about the matter, remembers being told by Slaughter's Tom Nelson that the issue of the necessary writ could no longer be delayed.

"Look John, if you don't give the all-clear now, you're not going to get this show on the road." To give an instant go-ahead, without further consultation, might have looked like rushing the Commission and so be diplomatically awkward. But there was no choice. It became necessary to cut short the informal dialogue and act.

"I said 'OK, serve it,'" John Fry remembers. "It was one of the most nerve-wracking decisions I ever made in my life."

In fact, matters proceeded smoothly to the next stage.

The Judge, persuaded of the urgency, heard the matter over two days, on January 5-6, and gave judgement the following Monday, January 9. The case was, in the opinion of some involved, quite unique, with the Judge being "talked through" the hitherto untested and sometimes tortuous conversion parts of the Act.

"It was like no other case that I've ever been in. It was like a tutorial," Nick Wilson remarked afterwards.

With their fingers crossed, the parties crammed into the Court to hear the Judgement on which so much depended.

The Vice-Chancellor first dealt with the underwriting, to the unalloyed satisfaction of Abbey National. Since the underwriters would not be "subscribers" in the sense of the Act, the arrangement did not contravene the relevant section.

On the free shares, Sir Nicholas kept the Court on tenterhooks, giving the Abbey party some heart-stopping moments. Eventually, prefacing his remarks with the words "doing the best I can with this very obscure statutory provision," he laid down that the scheme would be legal on the vital condition that the class of members entitled to free shares should be exactly the same as those eligible to subscribe for new shares. This called for some rapid changes, such as excluding from free shares foreign residents barred by their own laws from receiving the cash offer.

A court cliffhanger

On the third point, the Judge's ruling was more reassuring than Abbey had expected over what could have been a dangerous loophole. The effect of it was that it would not be possible for a smart operator to "park" large savings over the turn of the year and, having quickly pulled them out, thereby sacrificing membership and the right to vote and get free shares, then collect a percentage cash payment on the money. (The safeguard already devised against such manoeuvres - the obligatory retention of 1p in other unused closed accounts - was nonetheless retained).

A Court declaration on the lines of the Judgment was then made, effectively giving the scheme a more solid status of confirmed legality. The sense of relief was overwhelming as the group surmounted what was probably its most challenging hurdle. The Court cliffhanger had, for a while, put a huge question-mark over Abbey's planned future.

"It nearly killed us for a time," later recalled Sir Campbell, who was then all set to embark on his countrywide series of "road show" meetings.

Two days later the group unveiled its "Vote and Float" plan for a free shares handout, some £1 billion worth of extra shares for sale to members, and the ballot procedure, culminating in a special general meeting on April 11, 1989. The share benefits were for those who were eligible members on December 31, 1988, and who remained in membership until April 11. Special share-dealing facilities for the millions of members would also be provided.

Sir Campbell summed up by saying: "We intend nothing less than to unlock the value of Abbey National for the benefit of our members, and for the future." Of the change over itself, he added: "Mutuality has served us well in the past, but for us the concept is an outdated one."

Full details were to be sent to members in the transfer document in early March, along with voting forms for this largest-ever private poll.

Preparation of the transfer document - "the manifesto," as it has been called - was in the hands of a special team which laboured for months through long days, often into nights, producing the 87-page paper. So complex was the task that, with the need to liaise closely with the Commission, the Stock Exchange and others, the document ran through 30 drafts. Such testing experiences engendered a high degree of camaraderie among the group, which reported to John Fry and which had the nickname the "magic coterie."

From Abbey, the participants included Graeme Johnston, a Scottish accountant and legal graduate who had been pulled out of his audit job at a few days' notice in March 1988 to become conversion co-ordinator. Another was Ian Harley, also a Scot and the assistant general manager, finance, while colleagues including Douglas Carter, assistant general manager, corporate planning, and Phil Hallatt, a deputy secretary, took part at times.

Slaughters were represented by Nick Wilson and Tim Clark, together sometimes with Frances Murphy, while Stephen Box, a partner, and/or Ian Brooks, a manager, represented the accountants Deloitte. The meetings, held principally at Kleinworts, were usually hosted by John Williams and the younger Tim Wise. Those near the scene credit Ian Harley and Tim Wise with being joke-makers extraordinary who helped lighten the gruelling task.

The Vote and the Float. Sir Campbell unveils details of the conversion scheme, the timetable and the members' ballot.

As the first society to seek conversion, Abbey National had decisions to make without benefit of precedent on the shape of the transfer document. The statement was statutorily required to describe the scheme, its benefits and their recipients, the consequences of conversion, with forecasts of future activity, financial information and much more. This 47-page section would have sufficed, but the society decided to add background on recent industry developments, a chapter on "Advantages and Disadvantages of Conversion" and further material important to the Stock Exchange.

Combining simplicity with exactitude was no easy task and Tim Clark, obliged to change some sparkling sentence into legally tight wording, was occasionally ribbed as "Mr Turgid." John Williams, who would at times vanish to cope with other meetings, returning just as the sandwich lunch trolley appeared around one o'clock, was duly dubbed "our avocado and bacon man." Some sessions, such as the one in which the "show-stopper" poser concerning the Priority Liquidation Distribution problem was confronted, ran into the small hours.

Drafts were exchanged with the Commission, the great majority of whose suggestions were incorporated, often word for word. But certain differences loomed.

The Commission would have liked profit forecasts for some years ahead, which Abbey thought neither feasible nor necessary; instead it confined itself to predicting the outcome for January - June 1989, a slightly reduced profit. There was also discussion on the presentation of the "Advantages and Disadvantages" section.

To Abbey, certain radical or unwelcome comments from the Commission were known as "Exocets." When some of these were made on Fridays, the team would work through the weekend to come up with answers by Monday.

Phil Hallatt. As logistics planner-in-chief, he was responsible for organising the massive ballot of Abbey members and the follow-up special general meeting at London's Wembley Arena.

To the Commission itself, a Government Department of restricted resources, dealing with this and later processes in the Abbey conversion to the tight timetable involved, was considered a task so weighty as to slow the despatch of other work, as was later made clear.

Eventually the drafting marathon and the "verification" meeting, when all statements had to be backed with evidence, were over. The board endorsed the completed transfer document - the manifesto to the voters - and its statutory part received the Commission's formal certificate of approval on March 2 1989.

Tim Clark of Slaughters recalls: "I think the abiding memory is of a team that got on enormously well with each other. It couldn't have been done otherwise. It's easy to get on with people over a relatively short period, but it's a real test to get on with them over 18 months. There was never any problem. It was a very good combination, with the task very professionally done, but done in a very friendly atmosphere. You looked forward to a day."

One Abbey insider, speaking appreciatively of the advisers, comments in reference to Slaughter: "They didn't say 'You.' They said 'We.' They would remind us of something needing to be done by observing: 'We've got to do this and do that.' It was that identification with us that so pleased the Abbey people."

Among other things, the transfer document made clear that the fixed issue of free shares would number 100 and that the extra shares, to be put up for sale to members in June, would be priced between 120p and 160p. Thus all members would receive value of £120 - £160 through the free handout even if they did not subscribe for the favourably priced extra shares.

The transfer document went to print at the beginning of March and was published a few days later when its despatch began. Around that time the drafting team marked the completion of this task with a lunch at theatreland's "Mon Plaisir" restaurant. A certain amount of peach champagne was consumed, along with other items, and the party only left when its table was urgently required for evening diners.

Abbey National's main presentation of its case for conversion was in the transfer document. Much of this long paper was concerned with details of the planned scheme, financial particulars and changes in the building societies' environment.

However, the document spelled out in various sections, some statutorily required, some not, the reasons why a switch to PLC status was proposed; it also outlined the group's broad business approach for the years ahead.

In the obligatory statement on Abbey National after Conversion (Part IV) the document outlined the "future activities" proposed for the new PLC. "Following conversion, the board of the Company does not intend that there will be any significant change in the nature of the activities currently carried on although the board intends to continue the Society's expansion in certain areas of the personal financial services market. Abbey National PLC will remain committed to the Society's overall objective of providing high quality personal financial products and services at competitive rates in the UK.

"In particular, Abbey National plc will seek to: .... strengthen the Society's position in the UK savings and mortgage markets; .... and continue to develop as a more broadly-based provider of personal financial services in the UK."

Former treasury man John Williams. A key Kleinwort adviser, he helped host the meetings to prepare Abbey's transfer document, which eventually ran to 30 drafts.

It confirmed that "the great majority of the Group's income derives, and will for the foreseeable future continue to derive, from its core savings and mortgage businesses. In the face of increasing competition, the board is determined to maintain a strong presence in that market so that the Company can make the most efficient use of the large scale of the Group's operations and thereby remain in a position to meet customers' needs competitively. To help achieve this, Abbey National PLC intends to modernise and expand the distribution network (principally the branch offices and Abbeylink cash dispensers) and, in order to increase the Group's access to the mortgage market and to create a further opportunity for long term growth, to develop further the substantial Cornerstone estate agency network."

As to looking further afield, the document recorded that "Abbey National plc will continue the Society's expansion into other sectors of the UK personal financial services market. The Society has established itself as a supplier of insurance products and pensions products and has entered the money transmission [cheque book] market. The board believes that these sectors offer excellent and logical opportunities for long term growth. They are complementary to the savings and mortgage businesses and will help to increase the customer base by establishing Abbey National plc as the principal contact for customers for a wide range of personal financial services.

"Abbey National PLC also intends to continue the limited development of the Society's overseas operations. The Society has already established operations in Jersey, Gibraltar and Spain and is in the process of setting up similar operations in certain other EC countries. These will initially be on a small scale and will usually be operated in conjunction with local partners. Abbey National PLC will continue the Society's involvement in property development in the United Kingdom, principally housebuilding, on a selective basis."

In a later (non-statutory) section giving extensive background to the conversion project, the document pointed to restrictions on the activities of building societies, despite easements in their operating framework. "For example, building societies are currently not able to lend more than £10,000 on an unsecured basis to any one individual (except in the case of certain bridging loans), own more than 15 per cent of a general insurance company, operate outside EC countries or develop land other than for primarily residential use."

The further permanent limits under the Act on different classes of asset which may be held were also noted.

The passage then indicated where constraints were felt in the field of money and capital markets. "The Act also imposes constraints on building societies in the area of treasury operations. The range of relatively risk free investments in which building societies can deal restricts their ability to manage their liquid asset portfolios effectively and, in particular, to take advantage of opportunities to increase earnings yields on their liquid portfolios. The predominant market for liquid instruments is the inter-bank market to which access is more restricted as a building society. Banks are able to make markets and trade much more easily in the full range of instruments used for overall liquidity asset management and are also able to invest in corporate sector debt and foreign currency denominated government bonds.

"Additionally, instruments for hedging against rate and currency exposures and positions may only be used by building societies for the purpose of reducing risk of loss. Further, building societies are restricted in the types of wholesale instrument which they can issue and are only permitted to raise 40 per cent of their funds in the wholesale markets. Furthermore, building societies currently have no access to any form of equity capital."

A succeeding summary also included these points: "Building societies are subject to a number of restrictions which do not apply to companies which carry on similar businesses .... There remains the overriding point that, unless legislative distinction between the powers of building societies and those which apply to companies carrying on similar businesses is ended, building societies may not be able to take advantage of every new opportunity that may arise in the personal financial services market, thereby disadvantaging building societies and increasing the risk that customers will use other types of financial institution."

The transfer document also included a four and a half page section headed "Advantages and Disadvantages of Conversion." This part, which attracted some controversy based on claims that "disadvantages" might have been more fully stated, proceeded, after an introduction, with passages under the sub-headings "Advantages of Conversion," "Disadvantages and Other Considerations" and "Conclusion."

The introduction stated that the Board believed that conversion would "strengthen and enhance Abbey National's savings and mortgage businesses and other activities by allowing Abbey National greater access to wider sources of both capital and funding, and allow Abbey National more flexibility in determining the nature and scale of products and services to be offered to customers while maintaining high levels of customer service."

In more detail, the document noted as advantages of conversion the great flexibility of operations and freedom from the constraints of the building societies legislation. It then spotlighted the particular improvements anticipated for customers and the prospective share benefits - for customers it would mean more branches, improved facilities in branches, increased privacy for advice and counselling, more Abbeylink cash dispensers, reduced queuing and more efficient service.

"Furthermore, the proposed conversion of the Society provides an opportunity to recognise members' ownership of Abbey National. The rights relating to the free shares and the new shares will give Qualifying Members enhanced rights of ownership of Abbey National, both in terms of value and control (within the different statutory framework)."

The advantages claimed were further spelled out under the

sub-headings including "Flexibility in range of products and services," "Ability to raise permanent capital" and "Treasury operations." Under "Recognition of ownership", the passage outlined the voting, dividend, information and other rights accruing to Abbey members becoming shareholders in the successor PLC.

Under "Disadvantages and Other Considerations," the documents noted the eventual possibility of a takeover of Abbey National PLC but recalled that there would be a five-year "protected period" in which no single holding could top 15 per cent. It pointed out also that deposit accounts with the PLC would not carry the "trustee status" enjoyed by savings with building societies.

On interest rates, the document said: "Some members have expressed concern that, following conversion, Abbey National plc will be forced to concentrate on making profits and that this will affect detrimentally the interest rates offered to savers and charged to borrowers. However, it will be in the interests of both Abbey National plc's shareholders and customers that it continues to offer competitive interest rates. It is the competitive environment in which Abbey National operates which largely determines interest rates for both savers and borrowers and this environment will remain the same whether Abbey National is a building society or a PLC."

The section concluded in these terms: "The Board has considered very carefully whether Abbey National should convert to PLC. It has come to the conclusion that conversion is the best way to secure the long term future for Abbey National and its members. The benefits to be gained from conversion are compelling and outweigh the disadvantages.

"The Board is recommending conversion so that Abbey National can continue to provide its customers with the products and services they want at competitive rates. Conversion will not affect the essential character of Abbey National. The Group will continue to concentrate on the provision of personal financial services in the UK. Above all, Abbey National will remain dedicated to its customers."

8

PLANNING IN MILLIONS

IT WAS not only in framing its scheme that Abbey's own commercial brand of general staffship was tested. As in all campaigns, logistics were vital and these and numerous other preparations went ahead under the various task forces. That chaired by James Tyrrell steered the financial planning, while John Bayliss and John Ellis respectively presided over those on communications and secretarial/legal matters.

With such a network, liaison was essential and this led to some key people having a place on most or all task forces. The conversion co-ordinator, Graeme Johnston, was in this category as were Slaughter's Tim Clark and Kleinwort's John Williams.

Stewart Gowans, the corporate affairs manager responsible for press, publicity and advertising operations, also shouldered the job of running a drafting group which, under the communications task forces, prepared the extensive conversion paperwork other than the transfer document. In the later stages, he also chaired a fresh mechanism for fostering co-ordination at working level, the so-called CLUG or communications liaison group. All agree that, beneath the formal frameworks, the bulk of work went ahead with informal liaison among those concerned. As Stewart Gowans remarked later: "The very fact of CLUG's creation led to a network of co-operation behind it that made things work."

On the systems side, Brian Leary, a chemistry graduate who had become a computer boffin, was made co-ordinator under Bob Knighton, general manager, management services.

At the topmost level the directors appointed some of their number to be available between board meetings or on matters not needing full board consideration. The members of this group, which held a supportive watching brief and was scarcely needed as arbiter of differences were Sir Campbell Adamson, Jeremy Rowe, Peter Davis, Sir John Garlick, Sir Iain Tennant and full-timers Peter Birch, John Fry and John Ellis.

Given the importance of logistics, a task group with this title was formed under Phil Hallatt, a deputy secretary. The work confronting it was daunting and not just because the quantities involved were often measured in millions.

Among items on its programme was planning the printing, packing, addressing and despatch of the bulky green-covered transfer document, with personalised, specially designed vote proxy forms and copies of a letter from Sir Campbell to 5.6 million members. This key package, the prelude to the vital ballot on the conversion scheme, was scheduled for posting in a phased pattern from March 6 - 16.

Comparable preparations for the production and despatch of documents to do with the free shares, and application forms for the extra shares offer, also figured on its agenda, along with much else. Phil Hallatt was responsible, too, for organising the special general meeting to be held in the spacious Wembley Arena on April 11 and for detailed plans concerning the preceding record-scale ballot. The role of independent scrutineers of the vote process was allotted to Deloitte Haskins & Sells, Abbey's auditors; it was one of several major conversion tasks performed by this accountancy group, now part of Coopers & Lybrand Deloitte.

The detailed arrangements for the huge poll illustrate just how much was involved in what might seem a straightforward operation. In this, as in much else, close contact was kept with the Building Societies Commission, which had to be satisfied the vote reflected the views of members eligible to take part. Preparations were closely monitored by Deloitte as scrutineers and legal advice was obtained both from Simon Robinson of Slaughters and Timothy Lloyd, QC.

One of the first requirements was that Abbey's "electoral roll," the list of those included in the ballot, should be produced in as perfectly up-to-date and correct form as was humanly possible. The society's computer records of account-holders were the starting point. As the number of accounts of all sorts — up to 10 million - well exceeded the 7 - 8 million total of individual members, the first step was to "de-duplicate" to identify individual members.

Following the spread in the 1980s of high interest, tiered and other special savings media, many members had several accounts and often mortgages too. From these had to be picked out the name of each holder. Also, when accounts in different designations - say "M. Smith," "M. E. Smith" and "Mrs M. Smith" appeared with the same address, it had to be established whether they represented one or more people. Through a process of computer vetting with manual investigation and checks an eligible voters list of 5.6 million was compiled.

Beyond this there were more than two million savings accounts of under £100, some very small, and a number of children's (minors') accounts. By law, neither of the latter classes held voting membership. Both were also to be excluded under the conversion scheme from receiving share benefits but they would later share a cash distribution totalling £5 million.

Brian Leary, described by colleagues as "unflappable," recalls how he approached the final production of membership list tapes between February 17 - 28, 1989, the latest feasible time for the task before the names were required by the printers.

"On February 17," he says, "we said: 'This is it,' and we extracted the relevant data from our main systems and started manipulating it into suites of programmes to produce, by the end of February, all the tapes. Our worst moment? It was at this time. The terrible thing was that we knew we couldn't get a second chance. It had to be right the first time. People were working round the clock to get it right."

In the end only a few hundred out of 5.6 million were wrong - a small batch was at first missed, while a few names were mistakenly included - but these errors were put right in time. It was even possible later to follow up notified address changes.

These details of members' names and addresses were then passed through Abbey's production staff to seven printing companies which placed them on the millions of proxy voting forms, pink ones for savers and green for borrowers. Two laser bureaux had translated the particulars into individual bar codes which were then added, so facilitating the later vote count.

Members were asked to tick the "FOR" or "AGAINST" boxes and sign the forms. Mailing firms put the transfer document with the proxy voting forms, a letter from the chairman and a pre-paid first-class reply envelope in each package. The use of bar-coding was a "first" for an operation of this nature.

Another innovation was a tracking system that allowed careful recording of the movement of batches of tapes and documents

Planning in millions

to and from the contractors and to the Post Office. Because of the tonnages involved, special arrangements for staged mailing over several days were made with the postal authorities.

The thick transfer document itself, whose production in 5.6 million copies required 450 tonnes of paper, was printed just in time for this process in the first few days of March.

It was a feature of Abbey National's programme that the society directly handled the ordering of these processes, with all the research, scheduling and quality control that went with them, through its Milton Keynes-based purchasing department headed by Derek Roylance.

The tight timetables of all these production procedures made tough demands on the print and direct mail manager, Sandra Kilbane, who handled the flow of documents to print contractors. An Abbey colleague remembers her being faced with a section of the transfer document, said to be days late because the lawyers had rewritten it. "She didn't scream," it was noted.

There were extra pressures because some deadlines were brought forward, or clarified at quite a late stage, as being March 1 rather than March 6. And a frantic rush over other arrangements occurred through misunderstanding whether the 21 days to the final receipt day for proxy votes ran until April 11, the special meeting day, or April 8. It was, in fact, the latter, which tightened the last day for the phased despatch of "voting packs" to March 16.

Planning the voting pack's production and despatch was just one peak in the handling of relays of communications to members, all in their millions, during the conversion process. Arrangements for all these, including letters from the chairman, leaflets and various forms, were organised by Abbey National's own staff directly with contractors avoiding the use of agents. The work proceeded under the close watch of the logistics task force.

Another key example of this process being used to good effect came when Abbey broke with established methods by itself directly ordering from suppliers the millions of share application forms later required for the cash offer in June. This contrasted with the traditional practice whereby the merchant bank concerned entrusts an issue's printing and mailing to one City printer, which sub-contracts most of it while keeping close control because of the high security and tight deadlines in question. By running this operation itself, Abbey again achieved notable savings while retaining tight control. Personalised forms with bar codes were once more used, with improved ink jet printing techniques which further shortened the process.

The forms were despatched, with the mini prospectus the Stock Exchange permitted for this mass issue, in place of the 82-page full prospectus. On this occasion, Abbey used 15 mailing bureaux, where 1,500 people packed 5.5 million sets of documents for despatch over three days in mid-June. As before, special arrangements were made with the Post Office.

All went well with these and other mailing operations. Derek Roylance afterwards reflected that the purchasing department had "broken the mould" for flotation exercises through its direct ordering and in other ways. He credits the organisation of supplier relationships and the sheer hard work and dedication of staff as "the qualities which pulled us through" despite the exacting schedules. Sandra Kilbane notes "14 nervous breakdowns" as another vital statistic of the pressured operation.

Having ensured that its new shares were exclusively provided to its own members, Abbey National went on to set up a special share trading facility for the recipients, most of whom would be new to stock market investment. The plan was masterminded by John Fry, who has explained that, of the five million new Abbey shareholders, "about 3.5 million would be first-time share owners and we therefore felt we ought to set up a sharedealing service that was simple, easy to understand and cheap, rather than leave them to find their way

Ian Brooks, a corporate finance manager at Deloittes, Abbey's auditors. He was part of the team who drew up the key transfer document.

Sir John Garlick. A former Whitehall mandarin, he was an active boardroom participant in the conversion decision.

through the maze of stock market dealing procedures." The preparatory work was in the hands of Malcolm Holdsworth, a former Abbey branch manager in the City of London (and now Abbey's manager of share-dealing services) who reported directly to John Fry.

Establishing the service proved an arduous business, the more so because the first long-discussed plan for an arrangement with Barclayshare fell through and a new partner had to be found. A successful deal was forged in January 1989 with Sharelink, a company controlled by British Telecom, and of which the other owners are the Birmingham stockbroker Albert E Sharp, and its managing director, David Jones. As the deals likely to flow from Abbey's 4 - 5 million new shareholders would be far larger than Sharelink had previously handled, it was necessary to set up and staff a major new centre for the purpose. A location was found in Aldridge, Birmingham, and detailed preparations were put in train.

The service was known as Abbey National Sharelink. Recruitment of several hundred employees and their training, obtaining premises and equipping them with the necessary computer and telephone installations, made the project an enormous operation.

Arrangements for handling big volumes of post, and for demonstrating to the Stock Exchange that the large expected turnover could be satisfactorily dealt with, were other key tasks.

One of the hardest jobs was to estimate what scale of business the service might have to transact. Nobody could tell how

Graeme Johnston, Abbey's conversion co-ordinator. A Scottish accountant and legal graduate, he had the responsibility of linking all the task forces.

Stewart Gowans, Abbey's corporate affairs manager responsible for all press, publicity and advertising. He chaired the so-called CLUG (Communications Liaison Group) through which all public pronouncements about the conversion and flotation had to be cleared.

the new shareholders - up to 5 million of them - would feel about keeping, or swiftly selling, their holdings. Estimates put the potential volume at up to a peak of 250,000 bargains a day or - allowing for quieter days - maybe one million separate deals in the first two weeks after flotation. It was thought that, allowing for a rapid fall-off after the initial surge, the first three months of trading could see some two million transactions, about half-and-half in sales of free and bought shares.

In the event, turnover through Abbey National Sharelink and other brokers worked out at less than the forecast maximum as former members showed a taste for keeping their new shares.

While the service did not reach the peak volumes that had been thought possible, share trades through it from mid-July to the end of November did number a very substantial 572,000 bargains and accounted for an estimated 60 per cent of all transactions in Abbey shares during that time. The commission charged on small deals was a modest £12 + VAT. Always expected to be a subsidised facility, the service cost Abbey National some £5.8 million.

Abbey National Sharelink was essentially a postal service angled at small-scale sellers, though it also included a telephone buying facility. It was intended to run from July 12, the day of Abbey's stock market debut, until September 30, though it was later extended to November 30 and has now been succeeded by the permanent Abbey National Share Dealing Service in association with the same partners.

The Abbey National Sharelink service was presented to members in an illustrated brochure on stock market dealings which was distributed in April and May of 1989. It was enclosed with the so-called "Free Shares Form," another important "mailing" which asked members to confirm their entitlement to the handout with their exact names and addresses.

In addition to making arrangements for this service, Malcolm Holdsworth also played a large part in Abbey's negotiations with the Stock Exchange over various novel aspects concerning the share certificates and their handling.

One important innovation was that Abbey National shareholders would receive definitive share certificates in time for the first day of dealings. This was instead of the more usual issue of a renounceable letter of allotment, replaceable by a later certificate. The large number of free shares being issued made this a particularly welcome arrangement.

Furthermore, the Abbey National certificate had a new design, with a 'SOLD TRANSFER' section on the reverse. This made it easy for holders to sign the form and send it to a broker (including the Sharelink service) if they wished to dispose of their shares. This type of certificate was specially planned with the Stock Exchange for ready handling through the latter's settlement system and the arrangement - to be repeated in the later Water and Electricity privatisation issues - was jointly announced by Abbey and the Exchange.

The certificate could also be used to switch ownership from the single allottee to other holders, including charities. In particular, the title could be changed to a joint-name. This facility was popular with wives who had been excluded, by being second-named holders in joint accounts, from themselves receiving shares.

Other "firsts" worked out for the Abbey issue included a direct debit facility to an account with the society so that applicants allocated fewer shares than they put in for should not have to wait for refunds.

To act as the receiving bank for its share offer (a function it was not permitted to perform itself), and as permanent registrar of its shareholder list, Abbey National chose Lloyds Bank. Others of the big High Street banks which specialise in the services also tendered but Lloyds was picked for its reputation as the leader in the field. Lloyds' Bill Paine, who had built up his bank's expertise in registrar work, took part in the planning process.

When it unveiled the outline of its conversion scheme and the timetable for it on January 11, 1989, Abbey National also announced the introduction of an information office. Set up with a smallish staff under Peter Fisher as manager, this department was entrusted with answering the many enquiries, by letter or telephone, to be expected from members. These would be both about the meaning of the scheme and the position under it of individuals.

With assistance from a British Telecom reply service operating on its behalf, the information office handled many queries with the help of standard responses. Given legal constraints which limited what could be said, the preparation of the wording of these was in the hands of a special "vetting group" including representatives of Slaughter & May, the City legal advisers, and of Kleinwort Benson, Abbey's merchant bank. Replies to queries to which a standard response was unsuitable were checked by the same group.

Up to early May 1989 there were 168,000 calls to the office, 25,000 necessitating answers in writing, and 17,000 letters, all of which were answered.

Planning in millions

As the volume of enquiries mounted, the information office had to be expanded. At the peak during the share certificates crisis in July 1989, the office was overwhelmed with some 1,000 or more calls a day. At earlier stages, there was some complaint that the office was difficult to reach as the telephone line was engaged.

Any enquirers raising objections to the scheme as foreshadowed in January were asked, in the following standard terms, to await the detailed transfer document: "I'm sorry, but we are here only to provide information, not to comment on the rules of voting or the conversion arrangements. It is up to you to decide whether to vote for or against the proposal after reading the transfer document that will be sent to you in March."

In step with all the logistics planning, there were numerous documents to be drafted, quite apart from the lengthy transfer document and other papers to do with finance and the share issues. For example there was the sequence of four letters from the chairman to members, the first two of them accompanied by question and answer leaflets, all, of course, needing printing in millions. There were also speeches to be drafted, including those for Sir Campbell's "road show" programme in early-1989.

In addition there were press enquiries, averaging 20 to 30 a day, to be answered, since conversion gained a high degree of newspaper coverage. Journalists were attracted by the subject's intrinsic interest, the millions of members - and so readers - involved and by the drama created by the opposition campaign against conversion waged by AMAF.

All this, and more fell under John Bayliss' communications task force, to the organising powers of the corporate affairs manager, Stewart Gowans, and participants in a drafting party he ran virtually daily for many months. Others in this group included Kleinwort's John Williams and Tim Wise, Slaughter's Tim Clark and Chris Saunders and, from Broad Street Associates, John Harben.

Harben, a lively public relations man and generator of good ideas - occasionally, even he was too bold for the least staid building society - worked virtually full-time on the project. Also from Broad Street was Jane Ageros, a Cambridge graduate and one-time teacher who specialised in drafting and in the delicate task of "clearing" wordings with parties concerned. In this Ageros, now on Abbey's staff as publications manager, is credited with having shown great gifts of "tact and wheedling."

None of this work was made easier by the fact that all

pronouncements, including public statements, messages to members and individual letters, needed most careful phrasing from the legal standpoint. They were vetted by lawyers in a further elaboration of procedures which led the project co-ordinator, Graeme Johnston, to joke, referring to the City lawyers, Slaughter & May that "everything we wrote was 'Slaughtered." Statements with any investment aspect needed clearance by Abbey's merchant bank, Kleinwort Benson.

The need for this extra special care arose partly from the requirement under the new Financial Services Act 1986 for Abbey to avoid appearing to give what could rank as investment advice. For this reason, the information office which the group set up in 1988, and much expanded in 1989, had not only to rely heavily on standardised replies in writing. It had also to operate under an investment authorisation from the Securities and Investments Board.

Additionally, the conversion provisions of the Building Societies Act made it necessary to avoid any lobbying for a "Yes" vote. All these factors made it the more vital that all statements from whatever Abbey source which touched at all on conversion should tally with each other.

John Fry has described the degree of constraint all this meant: "By law we were required to ensure that all messages given out by Abbey National - whether a radio broadcast, in an interview with a journalist or over the branch counter - were consistent. The reply to every single call and letter was vetted by a team of lawyers and merchant bankers to ensure that every detail of information given conformed to the statements made in the transfer document and to the [later] prospectus. The same team of lawyers and bankers had to 'sign off' every single piece of literature sent to members and indeed staff, every leaflet, every letter, every poster in every branch. The Building Societies Commission also saw and commented on all of these communications." Slaughter's Chris Saunders was much involved in checking answers by the information office.

Just how hampering these limitations were can be highlighted by a few comments and illustrations. One consultant experienced in large privatisations remarked: "I've never seen a company so much in the hands of its advisers." And Stewart Gowans recalls: "Every script, every sentence, every rubric, even three words on the outside of an envelope, would cause an hour's discussion and legal debate."

The problems of getting a consensus are illustrated by the question of fixing a title for the circular through which members were asked to confirm their eligibility for free shares. In a long discussion the lawyers objected to the implications of "Share Certificate Request Form," while the public relations people found "Validation Form" less than user-friendly. Eventually the unobjectionable "Free Shares Form" was agreed on.

There were various consequences of the legal constraints which took effect from the announcement of the conversion programme in January 1989. In the first place, branch staff were effectively prevented from discussing conversion with members lest the wrong thing be said. They tried to be as helpful as possible, but little more than routine assistance was permissible.

Plentiful effort went into explaining to staff up and down the country what conversion was all about, and what it meant for them personally in terms of available shares. While many managers were enthused by the future business prospects, there were signs some staff on occasion felt their bosses hardly understood the problems at grass roots level. This was particularly so in the turbulent aftermath of the lost share certificates catastrophe in July 1989.

It was also judged necessary, from the start of 1989, just after the qualifying day (December 31, 1988), for membership carrying entitlements under the conversion scheme to include a cautionary form of words on many documents.

For example, the rubric attached to the letter sent by Sir Campbell on January 11, 1989, to tell members of the "Vote and Float" plan, read as follows: "Issued by Abbey National Building Society, which is regulated in the conduct of investment business by The Securities and Investments Board. The information in this letter on voting and benefits is a summary based on the Rules of the Society; full details will be sent out in the Transfer Statement due to be published in March. This letter does not form part of any offer of any securities. Any decision on voting or application for shares should be made only after consideration of, and on the basis of, information contained in the Transfer Statement and prospectus to be published in due course."

A further result of the legal strait-jacket was that an effort to produce a "core case" - a punchily-written paper for Press and other contacts driving home the arguments for conversion - never came to fruition. It was attempted by the corporate affairs and public relations people but the Commission's requirement for "balanced" presentation meant that the "pro" case had essentially to rest as it was put in the formal transfer document, including its "Advantages and

Disadvantages" section. So the "core case" project was shelved.

One aspect of the conversion story which is widely felt to have involved problems was the long interval after the disclosure in March 1988 of the proposal to convert. Ten months then elapsed before, in January 1989, the society announced its timetable for the planned "Vote and Float" and outlined its chosen scheme, involving free shares.

Although preparatory work was being busily carried forward during this time, members and the world outside were left facing as many questions as answers.

To fill the gap Sir Campbell, who had conveyed the first news to members in a letter dated March 1988, wrote to them twice more, in July and November 1988. A further letter described the clear-cut plans unfolded in January 1989.

The July letter set out some of the thinking which had led to the decision to seek a change of legal form under four main summaries of argument. These were: "In order to meet customer needs we must be able to respond more quickly and flexibly to changing conditions." .... "We need to be able to raise extra capital more easily and economically." .... "We need to ensure an ample and steady flow of mortgage funds at competitive rates as a principal service to our borrowers," and .... "We need to be able to meet increasing competition from American, Japanese and European financial institutions in the UK."

A leaflet setting out some of the queries raised by members, with the board's answers, was enclosed. A further such leaflet accompanied the next letter in November, which was briefer and announced the coming programme of "road show" meetings the chairman planned in the New Year with members up and down the country.

The problem which emerged was that during the 10-month gap many members, as well as newspaper commentators, had a host of questions to which little in the way of answers was yet available.

Having, over the years, earned a reputation with the Press for being forthcoming and frank, Abbey was obliged, given the looming legal curbs, to limit what it said, meanwhile promising more formal statements later. As one close observer remarks: "Journalists couldn't understand, no-one outside could understand, the constraints. And the journalists attributed all kinds of motives to our lack of candour."

The situation was made particularly awkward for Abbey National by the fact that the ginger group opposed to conversion,

Abbey Members Against Flotation, was meanwhile conducting a vigorous campaign against the society's plan. Focusing on issues such as "mutual ethic versus profit motive," AMAF had been a stimulus to much discussion in the Press which Abbey people felt inhibited in combating.

AMAF's appearance on the scene was going to make the next two months - the period of the chairman's country-wide "Road Show" meetings - anything but smooth.

9

ENTER AMAF

OPPOSITION to Abbey National's project to go public was centred in the smallish AMAF ginger group, whose energetic campaign, inspired by mistrust of the new plan, attracted wide publicity and a measure of support.

Just six like-minded people came together to form Abbey Members Against Flotation following a letter to "The Guardian" from the man who became its chairman, Alex Leaver, a London borough councillor and former trades union official. Others among the initial half-dozen included Otto Hamburger, a retired businessman, Andrew Lewis, a journalist, John Collins, a local government officer, and David Chivers, a barrister.

But the man who perhaps played the role of chief mastermind in challenging the Abbey board was Alexander Sandison, a 72-year old retired scientific librarian, named as AMAF's vice-chairman and its press officer. The veteran of a successful lobbying exercise in the 1960s to stop the "Beeching axe" closure of a Croydon branch railway line, Alexander Sandison ran much of the campaign from his Bloomsbury flat.

It was conducted with all the paraphernalia of press notices, telephone briefings, newsletters and car stickers with the catch-phrase "Abbey Bank? NO THANKS."

At its most active, in May 1989, AMAF had no more than 1,405 members who contributed the cash towards its shoe-string operation. Despite this, it managed to mobilise a network of 25 organisers around the country. Altogether, thanks to the application and tactical skills of Alex Leaver, Alexander Sandison and others, the pressure group made a large stir. It substantially contributed to -

indeed did much to provoke - an intensive dialogue on Abbey's plans in the Press, at the "road shows" and finally before the Building Societies Commission. The whole effort was prompted by regard for Abbey National's time-honoured mutual status and by a sense of obligation to subject the society's plan and arguments to the most searching scrutiny.

AMAF swung swiftly into action after the board's decision to recommend switching to corporate form. At the society's 1988 annual meeting a month later, on April 27, it obtained Sir Campbell Adamson's permission to place its "Open letter to Abbey National members" on every seat.

Words used in this foreshadowed part of its coming campaign: "As a mutual society, the Abbey National is run for the benefit of its members. If it becomes a PLC, it will be owned by shareholders and run for their benefit. We recognise the successes of the society in recent years and the greatly improved range of facilities now offered to members. But we do not agree that flotation is necessary if further benefits are to be achieved."

The sequel was a lengthy discussion about the conversion plan at the meeting although the subject was not on the agenda. Sir Campbell resisted pressure from the floor to give facilities to AMAF to circulate its views to the society's millions of members. However, he expressed willingness to meet the group's representatives later.

All along the board, to which AMAF's words and hardhitting campaign were often exasperating, set its face against treating the rebel group as speaking for more than its own small membership. Abbey explained that it would be wrong for it to give special treatment to one body of members over any other.

There was never any hesitation about refusing the distribution facilities asked for by the pressure group, "which wanted a free ride in our mailings" as one Abbey executive put it. But there are signs that there were on occasion more than one opinion within the society as to how AMAF should be handled in other ways. For instance, there were some doubts about the policy of refusing to give enquirers AMAF's address and telephone number.

By a tragic irony Alexander Sandison collapsed when speaking at Abbey National PLC's annual meeting in April 1990 and died soon afterwards. Only two months earlier he explained AMAF's strategic approach, which was to focus on the merits of the conversion issue and to campaign for a full debate on the matter.

"We objected to conversion," he said. "But, equally important, we felt the members ought to be given the arguments on both sides fairly and objectively, so that they could make up their own minds." Submissions which AMAF later made to the Building Societies Commission were relevant to the latter aim.

One of the rebel group's problems was the difficulty of getting its views across to the millions of members who would take part in the vote on the PLC plan. A direct mailing was out of the question on cost grounds alone; the £1 million plan involved was vastly beyond the resources of AMAF which, anyway, lacked a list of members' names and addresses.

Press conference for AMAF (Abbey Members Against Conversion), the small ginger group which, in the words of Abbey itself, "gave us a hell of a run for our money." The late Alexander Sandison (left), a retired scientific librarian, was vice chairman and Alex Leaver, a former trades union official, chairman.

Newspaper commentators were naturally interested in AMAF's activities - not least in the "David and Goliath" aspect of the confrontation. Their reports in turn stimulated interest in the opposition's efforts.

AMAF leaflets were distributed to the 5,000 people who contacted the group and in other ways such as by distributions at branches. One leaflet, launched in June 1988 with the title "It's Your Decision" carried a cartoon of a well-nourished figure with a briefcase marked "Bank PLC" coming between a young couple and walking off with the Abbey roof logo the young pair had been holding. The text set out 10 major differences, as AMAF perceived them, between building societies and PLCs, to the formers' advantage.

Among the contrasting pairs of propositions, under the headings respectively of "Mutual Building Societies" and "PLCs," one set read: "As a borrower or saver with the Abbey National, you are a 'member.' You own it and you have a vote." And "PLCs are owned by shareholders and not by the savers or borrowers. The more shares the more votes."

Another set ran: (For mutuals) "Interest rates are the most favourable to members that market conditions permit." and (For PLCs) "Interest rates are fixed to make high profits and to be as unfavourable to borrowers and lenders as market conditions permit." Abbey always strongly contested the latter argument, insisting that the market made rates competitive whatever the lender's form of organisation.

The front page of one of AMAF's leaflets lobbying against conversion. With their minimal resources, this was one of the few documents that AMAF was able to produce.

After a meeting which he and Alex Leaver had with Sir Campbell Adamson, Peter Birch and John Ellis on June 27, 1988, Alexander Sandison said the Abbey chiefs were adamant that the opposition group would not be given a platform to air its views. Its leaflets would not be distributed with Abbey communications, nor would it be allowed a right of reply at the planned "road shows" to explain the conversion scheme to members.

In a written record made later, Alexander Sandison said his group had been hoping to discuss ways of co-operation in presenting the facts to members. "All its suggestions were, however, turned down flat, even the request to be allowed to put factual leaflets in the racks in branches."

On the Abbey side, any sympathy with the pressure group was now ebbing. One senior figure in the society later remarked:

"We'd been through a very long process in working out all the arguments before the board had reached their conclusion - in favour of conversion. And here were these upstarts, AMAF, who were immediately saying 'This is wrong,' and putting these sort of leaflets about."

AMAF's next major initiative was to submit, in September 1988, a requisition drawn up under the society's rules for the summoning of a special general meeting of Abbey's members. This was backed by 110 signatures and a cheque for £5,500 as the statutory deposit which had been largely financed by loans from members.

Resolutions proposed to be moved at the meeting regretted that arguments for conversion had been presented unaccompanied by those against; instructed the directors to recognise AMAF and expressed concern at the level of costs incurred on conversion plans before members had been consulted.

Had the requisition been successful, Abbey would have been forced to circulate to its millions of members a notice of the meeting setting out the full resolutions. "We also took care to see the resolutions included our address," Alexander Sandison later remarked. Circulation of AMAF's address in this way would have achieved one of the pressure group's principal desires in giving the millions of Abbey National members a contact point with it.

Abbey National rejected the requisition on legal grounds after consulting its own and other lawyers. On October 7, Sir Campbell, with Peter Birch, Charles Wilson, Abbey's chief solicitor, and Slaughter's Tim Clark, met Alex Leaver, Alexander Sandison and David Chivers to relay their decision. The legal ground for the rejection was spelled out in more detail later to Alex Leaver.

It was explained that each of the resolutions would have been ineffective because it conflicted with the provisions of the society's rules, which conferred on the board the power to direct and manage the business, and the right to exercise all powers of the society which were not, by statute or the rules, required to be exercised in general meeting. Thus the members were not, under the rules of the society, able to instruct the board how it should exercise its powers. As an AMAF representative summed up: "They said: 'The meeting cannot direct the board.'" The deposit money was returned.

Some of the background to AMAF's application for a special general meeting lay in a Commons debate on July 27, 1988, before the conversion regulations made under the Act [The Building Societies

(Transfer of Business) Regulations] passed into law. In the course of speaking on the measure, Peter Lilley MP, then Economic Secretary to the Treasury, replied to a suggestion from the Labour MP Chris Smith that "societies should be obliged to circulate the views of members opposed to flotation."

The Minister then said: "I do not believe that proposal is either necessary or practical. The regulations and the commission together provide powerful safeguards against a society tempted to put only partial or one-sided information to its members. It is not reasonable to require a society to circulate all its members with the views of every opponent, at any length and regardless of cost."

"However," the Minister went on, "it is worth noting that the Building Societies Act 1986 requires that if a group of 50 members propose a resolution at the [Annual General Meeting], the society must circulate not only that resolution but a copy of a short statement up to 100 words to all members qualified to vote, provided that the resolution and statement are not frivolous and would not damage confidence in the society. Therefore, a small group of members can have their views circulated to thousands or even millions of their fellow members."

He added: "A group of 100 members can also requisition a special meeting of the society if they think fit."

It was the latter point which AMAF followed up in its move although its proposed resolutions proved unacceptable on legal grounds. AMAF later maintained that the Minister's remarks "do not exclude co-operation with a properly constituted organisation with hundreds of members, although they were frequently quoted by [Abbey National] directors as though they did exclude it. Such co-operation in presenting arguments which a board has a duty to provide but does not agree with, would seem particularly valuable."

The latter comments, in a paper written about AMAF by Alexander Sandison after Abbey's conversion had gone through, are no doubt contentious and would be disputed by Abbey. However, they have some relevance to the continuing issue of how effect may best be given to the obligation which, in the eyes of the Building Societies Commission, a would-be converting society has to present to members both sides of the case.

With such a sequence of newsworthy doings, and with its frequent statements on the conversion question which concerned millions of people being widely reported, AMAF had, within a few months, secured a well-recognised position in the public eye.

"The media were extremely helpful," Alexander Sandison recalled afterwards. "I spent many afternoons on the phone." He was grateful for the interest of leading family finance writers. Indeed, his criticisms of Abbey's plan had first been highlighted in an article by Lorna Bourke, family money editor of "The Independent," when he gave notice of questions he hoped to raise at the 1988 annual meeting. He regretted, though, that coverage was largely confined to the financial sections as distinct from the more widely read general pages.

AMAF's campaign was not only extensively and largely sympathetically reported in the Press; its professionalism was noted elsewhere. "AMAF were extremely clever," recalls Abbey's corporate affairs manager, Stewart Gowans. "There was no learning curve in AMAF in terms of PR. After his Beeching branch line campaign, Sandison had, from the very beginning, as good a media list as we had. And he would spend all his time talking in an unfettered way to the Press."

It was one of Abbey's considerable worries that, while it was itself legally constrained by what it could say publicly in favour of conversion, the opposition group was under no such restraint in ventilating its views.

In its first few months, AMAF had collected a number of notable people as members, including university dons such as Professor Barry Supple, an economic historian and Master of St. Catherine's College, Cambridge, and Aberdeen's Professor Robert Perks, an accountancy expert.

In December 1988 the pressure group followed up the entitlement which Peter Lilley had pointed out for a sufficient number of members to propose resolutions for a society's annual meeting and have them circulated. It put up, well in advance, further resolutions for Abbey's 1989 annual general meeting on April 26.

AMAF went on to nominate seven people to oppose those directors coming up for re-election to the Abbey board. In addition to Alex Leaver, Professor Perks, Professor Supple and Elizabeth Stamp, the Oxfam information officer - and granddaughter of Lord Stamp who had once chaired Abbey Road Building Society - it named Thomas Lines, an Edinburgh lecturer, Clive Clark, a City accountant, and Christopher Bazlinton, a former Abbey employee.

The Abbey directors whose terms then fell due for renewal, and who were being rivalled by the AMAF list, were Sir Campbell Adamson, Richard Baglin, John Bayliss, Peter Birch, John Fry,

Michael Heap and Jeremy Rowe. There was more controversy when Abbey, in its turn, criticised the suitability of the AMAF nominees for their proposed role.

AMAF then achieved part of its long-desired object of communicating with all Abbey members because its resolutions, touching on what it considered "aspects of the conversion issue which the board had not seen fit to mention," were, like its candidates' election statements, duly distributed with the notice of the annual meeting.

The pressure group was incensed that the 15-day gap between the April 11 special meeting which was to decide Abbey's future and the later annual meeting meant that its statements for the latter would hardly reach members before they voted on conversion. Abbey denied any Machiavellian intent in this timing.

In the end, AMAF was to be defeated by almost 3:1 on its resolutions at the annual meeting, for which balloting was much lower than for the special (conversion) meeting, and to fail by wide margins to get its board candidates elected. The fact that its proportionate vote was less dwarfed then than was the opposition in the main conversion vote may, however, mean that the circulation of its views had had some effect. Records show that 40,000 Abbey members picked an AMAF candidate as a proxy in the annual meeting votes.

The group continued to fight its corner throughout the spring road show programme and in the later stages of the conversion process, particularly before the Building Societies Commission in May.

It stoutly defended the case for the mutual ethic, also focusing strongly on the "balanced presentation" issue - it did not feel Abbey had sufficiently brought out the disadvantages of conversion - and other aspects it thought worthy of comment. The retrospective survey of AMAF's own activities, prepared in July 1989, says: "AMAF believes that in reality the majority voted for free shares and the better branches featured in the media and advertisements."

The group, which had no political affiliations, was wound up in October 1989, three months after Abbey's conversion went through. The final annual report, by Alex Leaver as chairman, recorded satisfaction that 5,000 members had contacted the group and 300,000 voted against conversion. "For that alone our campaign was worth the tremendous effort so many AMAF supporters put into it ... We could gain no financial reward if we won. Perhaps the real lesson of the flotation is that a good bribe always wins a good argument."

Alexander Sandison, who was the inspiration of much of the protest group's work, outlined some of his own philosophy, first recalling his earlier campaign against closure of a branch line through the Croydon Transport Users' Association. "I've always been interested in standing up for the rights of the common man," he said, "particularly against, not the 'Establishment' necessarily, but the big boys. I was brought up in the days of the Beveridge Report [on social security, in the 1940s]. I believe that the role of government is to do things for the ordinary individual which he's unable to do for himself and which the vested interest is unlikely to do for him."

As to the AMAF campaign, he said of Abbey National's conversion plan: "It was a shift from mutual ownership - ownership by the people, the borrowers and lenders for whose benefit one hoped the society was run - to a PLC, which was to be run for the benefit of a third party, the shareholders." These remarks illumine much of the thinking behind the philosophical opposition a minority of Abbey members felt towards the conversion plan.

In a retrospective look after everything had been settled by the successful conversion, views in and around Abbey itself were mixed on the subject of the dissident group which had fought for the contrary view.

The comments from Abbey people and their advisers ranged

Another cartoonist's view depicting the tide of mail that all Abbey members received. Each large-scale posting cost £1 million.

AMAF made good copy, so the cartoonists had a field day. This one depicts the AMAF/Abbey confrontation.

across the spectrum. "They gave us a tremendous run for our money .... We mishandled them: we effectively froze them and that didn't help with the Press .... Theirs was an emotional appeal .... Some of their claims got cranky" .... It became rather a personal crusade to do us down on every single thing, to harangue us and not see any of the positive points in Abbey National. It became a slanging match from their point of view and I think they lost their credibility."

Sir Campbell views AMAF's campaign with the magnanimity of the victor. Referring to some advice to him "which was very stridently - if you can be strident in silence! - against giving them any help at all," he later said: "I got increasingly worried about this. I may have been a bit weak and I think I should have overruled and said: 'For goodness sake, it'll pay us to look as though we're being a little helpful now and again.' I would never have circulated their statement. But I would have liked to have bent over a bit to help them in ways which I think would just have avoided the criticism."

Alexander Sandison himself said in February 1990, referring to AMAF's campaign and the vote against Abbey's conversion: "The Abbey kept saying our membership was infinitesimal in relation to the membership as a whole. Of course. But bearing in mind that we were a party of six, with no help officially at all, accumulating 300,000 votes against conversion at the end - we consider that quite creditable."

Although AMAF lost the day, its campaign was one of the most conspicuous aspects of the whole conversion process, not least during the chairman's "Road Show" meetings.

10

ON THE ROAD

ONE OF the high spots of the conversion process was the "road show" programme of 17 meetings with members which Sir Campbell Adamson and Peter Birch held up and down the country over two months from January 12, 1989, from just after the announcement of the plan's outline to the time of its formal submission to members in the long transfer document.

It was a unique kind of travelling circus of top people, with an attendant cast of lawyers, publicity aides and touring vans bearing display material and complex communications gadgetry. Because, for the first time ever, a corporate change was dependent on the vote of a five million-strong membership, nothing quite of this kind had ever before been attempted.

The high-level panel has been described as: "our Gardeners Question Time roving team." Electronic briefing equipment, transported from place to place, allowed the platform party to be prompted on answers to obscure questions by backup staff via screen messages.

As the top team constantly set forth from London for a new venue, the support caravan rolled on round the country in preparation for the next fixture. One organiser describes how "our roadies and our waggon full of gear would pack up and decamp from one site to set up nights later in another."

Altogether, some 4,500 members came to these events, which were usually held in city hotels around 6 o'clock in the evening and were preceded by a "meet the bosses" opportunity for local staff. Attendances averaged 260 but reached a thousand at one get-together. Meeting sites ranged from Belfast to Brighton and from

Glasgow to Cardiff, with two crowded sessions in Central London, the last at the Park Lane Hotel in the West End. The chairman and the chief executive, who were at every gathering, were accompanied on the platform by either John Fry or John Ellis and often by a regional advisory committee man as chairman. The atmosphere throughout the sessions varied from occasionally mellow through unsettled to stormy.

The road shows were generally perceived as being to drum up support for the conversion scheme. Certainly they were a forum for the society's chiefs to explain the reasons for the PLC plan and to answer questions. They were intended to give members the chance to have their say, to bring out a feedback of views, including opposition - and they did. "They gave a public face to criticism," one adviser said.

The trend of questioning was mostly critical and majority feeling in the audience often hostile. This was despite the supportive presence of many local Abbey staff, whose presence was occasionally derided as a "plant."

In a sense, it was to be expected that the people attending would be those who were concerned rather than supportive. For to turn out on a dark winter's evening, members would probably have had to feel disquieted either on the principle of changing the society's mutual status or on personal aspects such as the exclusion of joint-account holders.

This led an adviser to comment later that, in holding the meetings, Abbey National was on a "hiding to nothing - it couldn't hope for anything but a hard ride." As was to be proved by the later heavy vote in favour of conversion, the silent majority of supporters largely stayed at home during the road shows.

The AMAF pressure group closely marked the Abbey panel's progress with the help of its regional network. Through its leaders, including Alexander Sandison, the vice-chairman, the group pressed for time to state the opposition case at some length at the meetings. At the second gathering, at Newcastle in mid-January, Alexander Sandison was backed by a show of hands from the audience in claiming the floor to make a full statement and Sir Campbell conceded this. In according speaking time, the platform sought to treat the AMAF people as on a par with other individual members.

Although AMAF's presence loomed seemingly large at the road shows, most members who spoke were unconnected with the protest group. Sandison explained that while an AMAF representative spoke at all the meetings, nearly all the questioners were unknown to AMAF beforehand.

AMAF usually handed out copies of the group's "It's Your Decision" leaflet before the meetings, with a special insert prepared for the road show series. The latter stressed the board's "legal duty" to give the arguments for and against conversion fairly, and raised other points including alleged disadvantages of operation as a bank.

A fresh note was distributed at the last road show in London. Clearly, many members arrived at the sessions with very real concerns - after all, criticisms of conversion had been well ventilated in the Press - and may have been prompted by AMAF's literature to raise specific questions.

One Abbey organiser remembers craning to hear what was said as Alexander Sandison held an impromptu press conference with enquiring reporters as members assembled for a road show.

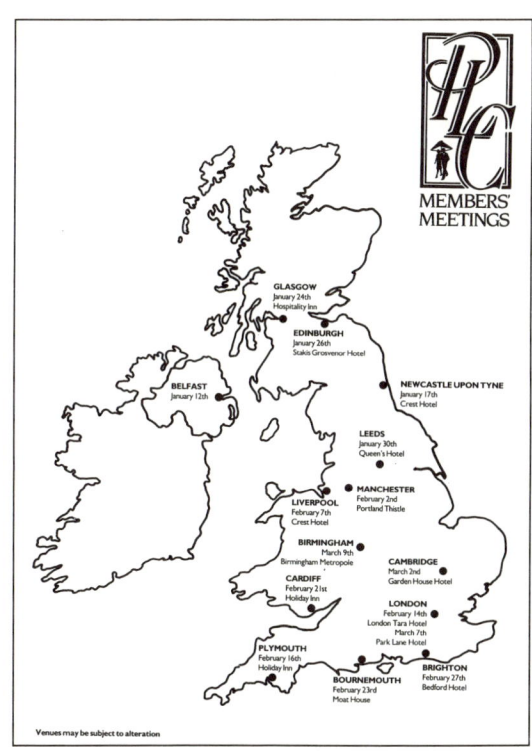

On the road. The map shows the chairman's "road show" itinerary. Meetings at Bristol and Derby were added.

A typical format of a road show meeting would be a speech by Sir Campbell, followed by one from Peter Birch explaining why the board was recommending the society's conversion into a public company. The speeches followed much the same pattern at each gathering. In retrospect it can be seen that they broadly mirrored in miniature the more detailed case as it would be set out in the coming transfer document.

For instance, at one typical meeting in Leeds on January 30, Sir Campbell said he hoped members agreed "that what has made us stand out is our performance and our determination to keep ahead of the game." This had required vision: now they were recommending another forward move with the proposal that Abbey National become a PLC.

He then explained that this was because the group felt the need for more flexibility than it was allowed by the building societies' legislation, so that it could strengthen its position in the UK savings and mortgage markets and could diversify beyond its one main business into new products, services and territories. This was in order to make Abbey less reliant on a single and maturing market and to chart a successful future course in increasingly competitive and rapidly-changing circumstances.

A rigorous examination of the options open to the society had been conducted over two years and the PLC course had been chosen as the best. Supposed drawbacks, including an eventual risk of takeover and adverse effects on interest rates, were discussed but with reassuring comment.

Sir Campbell then summed up with words that became familiar: "We intend nothing less than to unlock the value of Abbey National for the benefits of members and the future."

A platform argument sometimes heard was that, with its building society structure, Abbey was in a competitive financial world "fighting with its hands tied behind its back." Another comment might be: "We are not trying to change our spots after conversion. We are going to improve our services to you, the members."

Real worries and serious concerns surfaced in the questioning. Characteristically, there would be pleas from the audience for assurances that members would be treated just as well after the changeover, when there would be "shareholders with their own axes to grind," and queries about how the new status would foster better service.

A speaker in Edinburgh, who won applause, roundly stated: "The benefit of mutuality to me is that I know the money I deposit in the building society goes exclusively to helping people to buy their own homes. If I want to lend money to a Third World country, I can buy shares in the Midland or in the NatWest. I am going to remain a member of a mutual society and I hope other members will remain with me."

AMAF's pressure was relentless. At the first road show in Belfast, Professor Robert Perks urged that the Abbey National chiefs had a duty to explain conversion's disadvantages. In Edinburgh, lecturer Thomas Lines, alluding to the free shares handout, quoted to applause the comment that "a bribe is bad enough; it is even worse to be bribed with your own money." Sir Campbell riposted by asking what would have been said if there had been no free shares for members.

A certain amount of opposition throughout the series came from those who felt discriminated against by the foreshadowed conversion scheme, including (usually women) joint-account holders who were excluded from share benefits. At many meetings holders of larger savings protested that the equal share issue failed to recognise their position.

The meeting in Edinburgh brought the Abbey National touring team its biggest disappointment and least sympathetic hearing, partly perhaps because the city is the home of many major mutual financial bodies such as Standard Life and Scottish Widows.

Speaking at this meeting, Thomas Lines made a number of points, one touching on experience with mutual status. "There is absolutely no doubt that in recent years the building societies under mutual ownership have been considerably more successful than the banks. They have competed much more effectively. We believe that this is because of their form of ownership and that is supported by the experience in the life insurance sector, as is well known here in Edinburgh, where the headquarters of several highly successful mutually owned life insurance societies exist."

Lines also reported a telephone call from a lady who had said there was disquiet among management staff as to what the future held. "She said the staff were not necessarily against flotation but against the repercussions of it." She had reported a staff member's comment to the effect that "'nobody was going to get out of the door of a branch without somebody trying to sell them something.'"

He concluded by saying: "The old service ethic, which was the basis of mutual societies such as the Abbey National, will be replaced by a sales ethic, perhaps not surprisingly when the chief executive of our society [Peter Birch] is himself a former salesman."

Apart from such criticisms, this meeting also produced its lighter moments. One speaker, recalling in cheerfully combative mood the historic antagonism between his clan and the Campbells, claimed: "We want no Campbells here," overlooking that the latter was the chairman's Christian name and not his surname.

Sir Campbell later recalled of this meeting: "I'd been telling everybody beforehand 'Now, you won't have any trouble with Edinburgh. It's a decent place, only 50 miles from Kinross [his own original home town].' But we never had such a difficult meeting again as at Edinburgh. It ended up with a young man at the back of the hall - I don't know whether he'd had a beer or two - standing up and pointing at me saying: 'We know you came from Kinross, and we're damned glad you left it.' So I had to swallow my pride about Edinburgh. It's funny, it was also there they started the campaign against TSB going commercial."

At the first London road show, which attracted 600 in mid-February, the chairman and his colleagues were also given a tough time. In a speech there, Alexander Sandison turned to the audience, asking: "Have they (the platform) put forward any arguments against flotation?" evoking many cries of "No."

The penultimate meeting at the Park Lane Hotel, London, on March 7 was the best attended of all, with people standing or cramming the balconies. It was often stormy. So congested was the hall that the chairman asked Abbey staff present to stand up to allow others to sit down. When quite a number did rise, there were unfriendly "Oh's," implying that those in question - many in fact managers from throughout the south-east - were management "stooges."

One point pressed on this occasion by Alexander Sandison was that,"as Abbey National had said it had taken a long time to decide whether to recommend conversion or not, there must have been very cogent arguments against." He added: "I would ask you how many of those they have given you."

The chairman himself answered the bulk of the questions throughout the whole series in the practised style of the long-experienced public man.

"He had gone out on the road. And in the main he was enormously courteous to people in the hall," recalls an adviser. "He really did argue and there were very few occasions when his irritability showed. He just sometimes got tetchy with AMAF because they seemed to be claiming whatever he said was wrong. And that kills debate."

Though feeling in the audiences was mostly negative, there

were occasions when sentiment seemed to favour the platform, and shouts would tell opponents to "shut up." On a few occasions meetings even closed with applause for the visiting party.

The whole experience of the road shows for Abbey National's chiefs is described by executives as "just like putting yourself in the stocks" and metaphorically being on the receiving end of tossed tomatoes. It was a punishing schedule. Indeed, before the series started there had been concern about the strenuous nature of the programme for those chiefly concerned.

Yet there were no regrets that the tour had been undertaken. "We could at least say: 'We have bothered to go out all round the country,'" John Fry remarked afterwards. Colleagues remember the chairman saying that he could not have looked members in the face if he and his colleagues had not conducted the whistle-stop tour.

The road show programme had been postponed from its earlier scheduling for October - November through a wish not to build up interest prematurely. Then, last-minute arrangements were briefly thrown into doubt since the Court case remained unresolved until three days before the first meeting.

Retrospective comments on the whole series included some complaint that members had not been personally invited and had been left to rely on local advertisements of meetings, along with notices in branches from around half-way through the programme. Advertising was somewhat stepped up as the tour advanced.

One non-executive director comments: "The staff in the branches really did get the message that we meant business [about conversion] and that the cosiness of the service offered at branch level was not going to alter, though it would be toned up with more technology."

Hazel Riley, who was in charge of staging the public meetings and is now Abbey's events and presentations manager, makes the point that the road shows had advantages in helping explain Abbey's case, not just to the members attending them but to local staffs and to the Press.

On a separate plane preparations were underway for the various financial arrangements for conversion.

11

A LICENCE TO BANK

BY SWITCHING to commercial form, Abbey National would become a bank. But to be so in the eyes of the law and to operate as a bank, it needed a licence (authorisation) from the Bank of England. Obtaining this meant considerable procedures with the special feature that Abbey was the first-ever building society applicant seeking the seal of approval to enter the banking sector.

Work went ahead as promptly as anywhere on this aspect of planning, for there was much to be sorted out. The aim was that the Bank should, in good time, signal its willingness to grant a licence, since under the Building Societies Act the Commission could not confirm a conversion until this matter had been cleared in advance. The licence itself would only be issued at the final moment when all other hurdles to conversion and flotation had been surmounted. Even so, it was clear the consideration process would take many months.

Abbey's request for a banking licence called for some special judgments by the Bank of England, familiarly known as the "Old Lady of Threadneedle Street." As Britain's central bank, the Bank supervises a flock of more than 600 banks, most of them foreign-owned. Since Abbey's situation as an aspirant bank was unique through the group being a major, but different, type of financial institution, the Bank's handling of the application was a first and a trail-blazing operation for it.

As it happened, Abbey's request arose at a time when certain supervision ground rules were being reshaped under the Banking Act 1987 and the new international "Basle" pact creating "level playing-field" conditions among banks worldwide.

The Bank had also to make its usual assessment by getting to know the applicant's general character. It needed, too, to satisfy itself about management and computer controls and to learn of the would-be bank's broad future business approach. Assuming it was then ready to give the authorisation, it would next have to fix appropriate ratios to ensure that the group would have the necessary capital base to operate in the riskier new world of banking. Preliminary studies on the Bank's likely requirements had been done by Deloitte, Abbey's auditors, who were also auditors to the Bank itself and advisers to it on certain banking matters.

James Tyrrell, the finance general manager (from 1989 finance director), and his colleague Ian Harley, the assistant general manager, finance, and group financial controller, held discussions with the Bank not long after the board's conversion decision in March 1988. They were accompanied by Deloitte representatives Stephen Thomas, a partner, and Peter Jeffrey, the senior manager concerned with Abbey's audit.

It was arranged that Abbey would commission Deloitte to prepare a full-scale "reporting accountants' report." This was a type of report provided for in the 1987 Act. With an existing bank, such a report would normally deal with some particular aspect of the business. Since Abbey was a prospective newcomer to the field, a very wide-ranging report was judged appropriate as a prelude to the Bank's processing the licence application.

The report was duly commissioned by the society with the aim that, when completed, it should be passed to Abbey's board in the autumn and from them to the Bank. The very detailed review, focusing on procedures, systems, strategy and more, was conducted by a team led by Peter Jeffrey.

Its survey, the first of its extensive scope under the new Act, has been described as "the most thorough going over anybody had received at that time." It was crucial for the Bank's appraisal of Abbey National. Matters highlighted include the state of development of the computer systems, the form and flow of information to senior management, and structures such as a need for an assets and liabilities committee (ALCO) chaired by Peter Birch.

The Deloitte report, which came to hand in September, made certain recommendations, among them improvements on the systems side to capture information in the form required for regular reporting to the Bank. A programme of adjustments was begun.

Then, after its consideration by the board, the report was conveyed to the Bank, which held a meeting under a senior official with James Tyrrell, Ian Harley and a Deloitte team headed by a senior partner, Roy Foster.

Judging by later events, the outcome was satisfactory. For by December, after key particulars had been decided, the Bank indicated its readiness to grant a licence in due course. It was understood that Deloitte's team would return in the spring to produce a supplementary report on the improvements made.

Meanwhile, Bank officials had been getting acquainted with Abbey through visits to top management. There are one or two light-hearted recollections of exchanges with the Bank.

Ian Harley remembers asking the Bank official involved what had brought him this particular case, expecting an answer mentioning its importance. Instead the reply was "because Abbey fell in the A - D category. It wasn't that it was a put-down but it made me much more aware of our place in the scheme of things," says Harley, adding: "Still, we were bigger than the rest of his banking constituents put together."

As always, the Bank showed interest in the structure of Abbey's staffing. In particular, it enquired about that familiar banking character, the "Chief lending officer," a post unknown to the group, whose loan book (overwhelmingly mortgages) had little likeness to a clearing bank's diversified list. Lending was controlled by Abbey's own methods, including various management groups. There was much badinage, such as: "Where's the chief lending officer - under the table?" before an appointment with that title was made some time later.

In dealing with Abbey National's licence request, the Bank of England settled two novel and major questions in addition to deciding to grant the authorisation. One was where to set the "risk asset ratio," the required minimum capital in relation to assets, as "weighted" for riskiness. The second was how far the reserves, or net worth, which the new PLC would take over from the former building society, could count as capital in this context given the existence of a liability known as the "priority liquidation distribution" (PLD).

The PLD arises because the Building Societies Act gives former savers with a converted society a priority claim on the distribution of its assets in the unlikely event of the successor company being wound up. Each member's entitlement is based on the size of his holdings at the time of the changeover but is reduced by any later cut in his deposit and not restored by a subsequent increase. The PLD thus stands to run down quite rapidly through the normal ebb and flow of business. For instance, at the end of 1989, five and a half months' after conversion, Abbey's PLD had already shrunk by about a quarter: it was expected to be roughly halved at the end of 12 months.

The question was how far Abbey National PLC's starting reserves should be disallowed to cater for this situation considering that the PLD was so unlikely ever to be needed that it was not even accounted for as a contingent liability.

To disqualify all the initial reserves in the computation of capital would clearly be unduly harsh. It would mean Abbey having to raise every bit of its initial free basic equity capital by selling new shares. On the other hand, to allow all the £1,425 million reserves to count as unfettered base capital would pay too little heed the Act.

The Bank of England decided to recognise the PLD factor by disqualifying about half the initial reserves in the calculation of capital for supervisory purposes. The result was that Abbey National PLC could, from its first day as a bank - July 12, 1989 - count the other half of the reserves as capital. Moreover, since the PLD was expected to run down to a small figure within five years, the reserves at first disqualified would be steadily released back into the basic capital. This source of continuing free capital input is known as the "drip-feed."

An important consequence of the Bank's ruling was that the amount of cash Abbey would need to raise through its share offer to top up its starting reserves would be no more than about £1 billion. This was at the lower end of a span of previous possibilities ranging up to £2 billion.

The other vital matter to be settled with the Bank was what ratio of capital to risk-weighted assets should be set for the new PLC.

As it happened, Abbey was to enjoy one substantial advantage in the "weighting" process. Under the new "Basle" international agreement on standards of bank capital to be observed by banks worldwide, it had been agreed that mortgages, being relatively very safe assets, should only have a "weight" of half that for loans generally. The effect in the case of Abbey National PLC, whose asset book is dominated by mortgages, was that its total assets, to which required capital would be related, were usefully scaled down in the computation.

It is generally believed that the chief High Street clearing banks have minimum reserve asset ratios of round about nine in capital-to-assets, many other banks working to higher figures.

Building societies, by contrast, are required to hold scarcely half that figure. Abbey, as a newcomer to the banking sector and with a less broadly spread business range by activity and geographically than the typical clearer, could expect to be set a somewhat higher ratio than its new peers. The prospect of it diversifying into fresh and less familiar fields tended to point the same way.

On the other hand, the new PLC would be one of Britain's largest, most long-established and best known financial institutions with a good track record. The upshot is thought to have been that Abbey National PLC was prescribed a ratio rather higher, but not greatly higher, than the main clearers' figure. It would not be surprising if this were open to review after two years of the new banking status.

It should be noted here that the possibility of "buying out" members' PLD rights with additional free shares was considered. The aim would have been to release more reserves to rank as basic capital in the supervision context, so reducing the sum to be raised by the sale of shares. But the idea was shelved, as was that of taking out an insurance policy against the possibility of any claims on the PLD's ever arising.

Like other banks, the Abbey group in its new form would have to place a certain sum related to its deposits - and probably amounting to over £100 million - interest-free with the Bank of England. The consequent loss of interest is a cost falling on all banks under this "cash ratio deposits" scheme, which helps finance the Bank's own expenses.

With these matters thus settled, Abbey knew by December 1988 that the extra share offer it planned as a prelude to conversion to raise its capital to the Bank's exacting standards need not exceed £1 billion. Earlier on, there had been the worry that an issue no higher than this would hand too big a "windfall" profit to the subscribers. Once non-members were excluded from the extra share issue, concern of this kind diminished because all initial shares would now go, either free or for cash, to Abbey members.

James Tyrrell, the finance chief, had, for his part, successfully persuaded his colleagues that only the minimum necessary sum (close on £1 billion) should in fact be raised through extra shares. Any idea that the sum should be larger was further discouraged by prevailing City criticisms of the £1.27 billion TSB Group had raised on its own flotation in 1986.

Abbey National went public with 1.31 billion shares, of which

560 million (43 per cent) were created for distribution free to qualifying members, and 750 million (57 per cent) sold for 130p cash to those members who applied. The benefits of the society's reserves of £1.42 billion (reduced by conversion costs and a £5 million distribution to small savers and children) obviously went largely to the free share recipients. But some value from the reserves, in effect, also accrued to members who bought extra shares, since they saw an immediate profit over the 130p a share purchase price from the moment stock market trading started. The subscription price for the new shares would be fixed at this level, just before the big cash issue's launch in June.

Once shares are quoted on the Stock Exchange, the chance of a takeover exists unless special protection is created. Experience shows that bids are often made when a predator has first gained a springboard through amassing a share stake by market purchases.

The Building Societies Act provided anti-takeover safeguards for any newly converted building society so that it should have a breathing space to develop free of bid threats. The Act laid down that no shareholder could acquire an interest of more than 15 per cent during the five years after the changeover. This restriction had been duly written into Abbey National PLC's own articles.

But the board felt that, with the group's likely share profile, even this rule might not give enough protection. Shares would be thinly spread among millions of small shareholders, and even the large City funds, which would invest more substantially, would each only have a small proportion of Abbey's probable £2 billion-plus market worth. Thus, it would still be open to a resolute would-be bidder to build a holding worth over £300 million (15 per cent) and so acquire considerable influence over the PLC.

Accordingly, the possibility was explored of a more restrictive 10 per cent limit to last longer than the five years, unless shareholders voted otherwise through a special vote at a general meeting. After all, there was a precedent in the case of TSB, which had the yet tighter curb of a five per cent limit on holdings for five years, with an increase thereafter to 15 per cent, though the latter could be removed by a shareholders' vote.

This question was a matter for discussion with the Stock Exchange along with many others connected with the flotation, including the design of share certificates.

However, it is an important principle of the Exchange that trading in the stocks and shares it lists should be as unfettered as possible.

Through its brokers, Abbey sought the Exchange's agreement to a lower 10 per cent limit on individual shareholdings and the extension of some protection beyond five years. Ideas about "golden-style" special blocking shares, of the kind used in some privatisations, were also canvassed.

The first "road show" in Belfast, (left to right) John Fry, Sir Myles Humphreys, Sir Campbell Adamson, Peter Birch and John Ellis.

Kleinwort Benson Securities, in the person of a director J. I. M. (Jim) Hamilton, the head of corporate finance, took the lead in the matter through an arrangement made because of the Kleinwort group's other role as merchant bank adviser to Abbey National. S. G. Warburg's Rowe & Pitman, Abbey's lead broker, were also actively

Roy Foster, senior partner in Deloitte, Abbey's auditors. He was involved in drawing up "the reporting accountants' report" to support the application for a banking licence from the Bank of England.

Jim Hamilton, Kleinwort's head of corporate finance who briefed a 60-strong team over Abbey's underwriting.

A licence to bank

involved through its corporate finance head, the director Stuart Stradling. John Fry appeared at one stage, together with the brokers, before the relevant Exchange committee to press his group's case.

Eventually, however, in February 1989, the Exchange decided to stick to its principle of keeping restrictions on dealings to the minimum and refused to go beyond the statutory 15 per cent limit for

The Vote. Sealed ballot boxes are flown in with proxies from UK forces in Germany.

five years. These limits were accordingly adopted and in the transfer document Abbey included the warning that the 15 per cent and five-year curb "will, however, permit a person to have a significant investment in the share capital of Abbey National PLC which may,

Peter Jeffrey, a senior manager on the Deloitte team who were Abbey's auditors. He headed the scrutineers overseeing the massive ballot of Abbey members.

depending on the circumstances, enable that person to exercise influence over the Company (including its management)."

Many other matters also needed discussion with the

Exchange. The Exchange was kept closely in touch during the drafting of the transfer document, whose last section contained much of the matter also required in the later issue prospectus. Exchange officials readily agreed to the use of the "mini prospectus" for circulation to the millions of members: they would have liked the map included therein, showing the 677 branches, to be accompanied by a list of branches but ultimately allowed the use of the map without a written list.

An important piece of preparatory work which had been put in hand early by Deloitte was the production of a "long form report" on Abbey National. This is essentially a detailed study on a would-be quoted company to inform and "comfort" the merchant bank sponsoring the company for listing. The report also afforded useful material for the wide-ranging transfer document. Ian Brooks, a 28-year old manager from Deloitte's corporate finance side, did much work on the report and was also one of the "magic circle" which drafted the transfer document itself.

The need to familiarise investing institutions with Abbey National was not overlooked. For, although they would not be initial subscribers, these pension funds, insurance companies and other big investors were going to be the chief future buyers of the PLC's shares through the stock market. Some concern was at one time voiced by one of the brokers as to whether the institutional interest would be sufficiently lively if they were not given any "first pick" at the shares. However, Abbey's chiefs reaffirmed their decision to make the flotation share offer a members-only affair.

A series of institutional marketing and related sessions was accordingly laid on, mostly in the few days up to and around the mid-June share offer, to tell interested parties more about Abbey National. Some preliminary get-togethers had been held earlier, but the main programme was held up until after the Commission had cleared the conversion.

David Freud and Stuart Stradling, both directors of Warburg Securities, played prominent roles here, as did Kleinwort Benson Securities' director Jim Hamilton. There were meetings in the City with journalists and analysts, while fund managers attended gatherings at Abbey House over lunch or dinner. Both Rowe & Pitman and Kleinwort Benson Securities themselves held presentations for stockbrokers. Also, Sir Campbell Adamson and Peter Birch visited Scotland to talk about Abbey National to the financial community there.

Senior Abbey people played a notable part in various of these occasions, describing aspects of the group with the help of illustrative material. James Tyrrell was to the fore in this financial context, together with Peter Birch, chief executive and others. The Abbey team included Charlie Toner, chief of the branch network, who was an active participant. By all accounts, his direct manner and close knowledge of the grassroots of the organisation made him a particularly popular performer.

A considerable number of further important and complex financial issues had to be straightened out before conversion. One concerned the group's extensive wholesale money market borrowings, in the shape of floating rate notes, Eurodollar bonds and the like. By the normal process of such instruments' issue, a large chunk of them would often initially rest on the books of a City bank. The awkward question arose that such holdings, however short-lived, could run up against the 15 per cent limit on individual holdings which applied not just to Abbey's shares but also to certain loans.

James Tyrrell recalls that, as matters could have stood, the 15 per cent limit would have meant that "no one party, a merchant bank or investment bank, could issue an Abbey National bond if there was the slightest possibility that, for a nanosecond, it held all the issue" and so breached the 15 per cent limit on single holdings.

This conundrum was conveniently solved when Abbey National decided to conduct its Treasury business - its fund-raising and money-market dealings - through a separate wholesale bank subsidiary, Abbey National Treasury Services (ANTS). The 15 per cent limit, which applied to the parent Abbey National PLC, did not bite on loans raised by the Treasury subsidiary. ANTS, whose total assets at the end of 1989 were £7.03 billion, has as its main functions managing the group's assets and conducting a wholesale funding programme to complement the retail funding of the parent company.

Setting up the necessary arrangements, including obtaining for ANTS both a banking licence and the Inland Revenue's recognition of it as a "banking and trading company," was a big task for James Tyrrell, his colleagues and the group's advisers. The process involved discussions with government ministers and officials.

Another problem, also to do with wholesale borrowings, arose because the PLD, which was being charged on Abbey's assets, would be a claim ranking above those of the bond and note holders. Although the PLD liability was unlikely ever to come to anything in practice, it was necessary to renegotiate, or otherwise deal with, those

A licence to bank

loans whose holders stood, theoretically, to be adversely affected by conversion. The issues in question were those dating from before 1988, since the terms of later ones had PLD clauses written into them. One £500 million note issue, due to run to 1991, was dealt with through early repayment.

The cost of Abbey National's change of status was large but had always been expected to be. The transfer document estimated the bill at £80 million, made up of £45 million for the flotation (if the deal was approved and proceeded with) and £35 million for other expenses.

In the event, the 1989 accounts showed the cost, charged to the share premium account, at a good deal less - £66 million. The chief reason for the reduction was that, after the later disaster of the lost share certificates, Lloyds Bank agreed to a settlement which is believed to have been worth some £15 million.

Some highlights of the total are as follows: The long transfer document and its despatch, with related items, to 5-6 million members cost over £6 million; the prospectus for the cash issue of extra shares sent to members in "mini" form absorbed £4 million; various other mailings cost several more million pounds and over £12 million went on Press, TV, radio and poster advertising; spending on the road shows and associated publicity came to over £1.75 million.

As to the £975 million issue of extra shares for cash, the total sum receivable by Kleinwort Benson, the primary underwriters, the sub-underwriters and the brokers in connection with the underwriting, has been publicly revealed as £15.2 million exclusive of VAT. Other fees for certain City advisory services required about £3 million more. Further services, including accountancy ones, were another major item.

Given the £15 million or so of the settlement finally conceded by Lloyds Bank, it may be guessed that the sum originally budgeted for that group's services as receiving bank was not far from this figure.

The sharedealing service which Abbey National ran for four and a half months to help its millions of new shareholders involved a sizeable cost. Long expected to be a "loss leader," the service involved a larger loss than would have been in question if the maximum forecast volume of share sales had been reached. As it was, the service, whose setting up cost Abbey £1.3 million, incurred in addition an operating loss of £4.5 million.

As to the special general meeting at the Wembley Complex

which, on April 11, 1989, revealed members' verdict on the conversion plan, its costs left little, if any change, from £2 million.

With the "Road Show" meetings over and the voting packs despatched, attention now turned to the crucial ballot to settle Abbey's future structure.

12

VOTED THROUGH

WINNING members' approval for Abbey National's switch to company status had once seemed an unrealisable dream as it was feared that less than the needed minimum of more than 900,000 savers would bother to vote. Yet, as the crucial poll went ahead, the likelihood of a sufficient turnout, and a go-ahead for the change, was looking strong.

By the eve of the special meeting on April 11 which would reveal the verdict, bookmakers were quoting odds in favour of a "Yes" answer at 8-to-1 on. This was partly because the prospect of free shares was expected to swing support to the scheme. It was also partly due to a late trickle of Press predictions that the outcome would be favourable.

For a successful result from this biggest-ever private ballot, Abbey needed 20 per cent of the near-five million qualifying savers to vote with at least 75 per cent of those voting being in favour of the plan. Backing from a simple majority of borrowers was also required.

For some time hopes had been rising of a higher turnout than traditional building society polling inertia might have suggested. As many as 15 per cent of members had taken part in a lower-profile poll in 1987 on new rules framed by Abbey under the 1986 Act. In the light of that experience, Phil Hallatt, Abbey's chief planner of the conversion ballot and other logistics, recalls: "Personally, I had no lack of confidence in our ability to achieve a 20 per cent vote."

Indications from research carried out by National Opinion Poll (NOP) were also encouraging. For instance, a survey in early January 1989, before the free shares announcement, showed that nearly 70 per cent of customers expected to vote, although only 30 per cent were certain of this.

Looking back at such pointers to an easy clearing of the 20 per cent hurdle, Stewart Gowans, the corporate affairs manager, later reflected: "We didn't believe it; it seemed too good to be true."

Four days before April 11, Sue Stent, the market research manager, was reporting to Alan Dunstan, assistant general manager, marketing, that the latest survey pointed to a much more than adequate vote level, but with the favourable majority among savers seemingly close to the needed 75 per cent minimum.

The clock for the voting period itself began ticking from March 6, the start of 11 days over which the voting packs, including the proxy forms and the transfer document "manifesto," thumped through five million members' letterboxes. Completed proxies had to be in by Saturday, April 8, three days before the key special meeting in London's Wembley Arena at which members could, if they wished, vote in person.

The great majority of members - 90 per cent-plus - sent in their proxies by post. For those who preferred to deliver their own, Abbey provided sealed ballot boxes which, through a separate major piece of planning, were collected each night from its 677 branches. Some were transported from further afield, couriers regularly ferrying home those in the NAAFIs of Army and Air Force sites in Germany.

The big mailing was backed up by a multi-million pound TV, radio, Press and poster advertising campaign organised by Alan Dunstan's marketing department through the Capper Granger agency. The first theme of the campaign was that the voting pack was "On its way" and "It's in your interest to open it." The line then switched to "Don't Miss Out. Vote Now."

Capper Granger's vice chairman, Robert J Granger, explains that against the background of supposed member apathy and legal constraints, the approach was to generate around the poll a sense of excitement and importance. The idea was to distinguish the voting pack from "junk mail" and promote its arrival as an event to be eagerly anticipated and acted on.

The millions of returned proxy votes were counted on Abbey's behalf by the Milton Keynes firm Mailcom, which won the assignment after satisfying the society and Deloitte, the scrutineers, that it could handle the huge volume in time. Posted votes came back in an envelope addressed to the "Scrutineers Office," Milton Keynes, from where they were quickly passed to Mailcom, to which ballot boxes from branches were also transported.

On arrival at Mailcom, the proxy forms were checked that

they were signed and not defaced. They were then sorted into "For" and "Against" batches, and the particulars of each form read from the bar code with light pencils of the kind familiar in supermarkets. Details were fed into computers. Nearly four million votes were counted over 22 days by 60 people.

The arrangements, which were set up by Abbey National, were directly overseen by Deloitte who, as scrutineers, were required to vouch for the correctness of the whole voting process. Abbey people stayed in the background during the count, only having access to Mailcom under escort by Deloitte.

Deloitte's scrutineering work was described by Peter Jeffrey, the senior manager who ran it, as "in total hours much the biggest task" of the various roles the accountancy group performed in connection with Abbey's change of status. A 33-year old mathematics expert with a first from Hull University, he had for some time been his firm's team leader in its audit of Abbey National. He also played a key part in the production in 1988 of the reporting accountants' report in connection with Abbey's application for a banking licence.

The scrutineers' responsibility had begun long before the count and embraced everything from the first stages of planning for the vote in this unprecedented conversion procedure. Thus Deloitte had to monitor the construction of the de-duplicated "qualifying members" list and check the proxy form's fairness and legality. Printing arrangements for the proxies also came under its watchful eye.

Two former members of the accountancy group's staff, including Alan Cleveland, who had headed the registrar's department until his retirement, were brought in as consultants to the scrutineer team.

Since Deloitte is Abbey's auditor, it took special steps to underline the independence of its scrutineering role by putting in overall charge of it a senior partner from another part of the group. This was Ian Bond, whose normal responsibility was on the insolvency side. Deloitte was also legally advised on this work by Cameron Markby Hewitt, and not by Abbey's own City solicitors, Slaughter & May.

All this was for the sake of fair play not only being, but being seen to be, done. Phil Hallatt later commented: "The instructions I gave Deloittes really involved them in a way in which most scrutineers would never be involved."

No count of some four million votes could be trouble-free. A

Voted through

number of proxies came in unsigned, or signed with the second name on a joint-holder account. Returning these for correction was among the simpler of the sorting out tasks falling to the scrutineers.

Messages that proxies had been lost, defaced or "eaten by the dog" were common and 22,852 "duplicate" forms were issued. Only 172 "replacement" forms, sent to those wishing to change their vote, were requested.

A number of members could not resist a joke in using the right to nominate a proxy different from the chairman. Some voters named as their proxies members of the Royal Family, politicians (including Margaret Thatcher) and even Donald Duck. In practice proxies for non-serious nominations reverted to the chairman.

While the voting went ahead, arrangements were finalised for the special general meeting at Wembley Arena on April 11.

The choice of the venue for this key gathering, whose date had been fixed in mid-1988, gave Abbey considerable problems. The chief worry was that too small a site could be swamped with an attendance so large as to force a postponement of the meeting and vote result, putting flotation in jeopardy. Research had shown that two per cent of members - 100,000 - might turn up. This figure looked vastly too large judged by all previous experience, but still the selection of the meeting place was difficult.

Originally Central Hall, Westminster, with seating up to 3,500, was picked. But then over-crowding there which caused the adjournment of a London Life insurance group meeting led Abbey to think again.

The Albert Hall and Alexandra Palace in London were considered, as was the larger National Exhibition Centre in Birmingham. Eventually, after a decision that the meeting must be in London, Abbey's bosses, fingers crossed, fixed on Wembley Arena. Best known for hosting pop concerts, the Arena seats 12,000, while the adjacent football stadium, which was also booked, could accommodate a 30,000 overflow. Only by catering for such numbers could the planners safeguard against the chance of an improbably large personal turnout.

Saturday, April 8, marked the close of the proxy voting period. On Monday, April 10, the eve of the special meeting, Deloitte gave Abbey National its report on the tally of "For" and "Against" votes on the savers' special resolution, and the borrowers' ordinary resolution, to approve conversion. Only votes cast in person on April 11, over-riding any previous proxy, would need adding to yield the final totals.

Voted through

Until this point very few people at Abbey National had any direct knowledge of the way the vote was going. Yet already betting odds publicly foreshadowed a clear "Yes" outcome. The explanation of this seeming paradox is this.

Abbey's arrangement with Deloitte as scrutineer was that the latter should supply it with regular reports on how the voting was going, both in scale and direction. The particulars were given daily to Phil Hallatt, a deputy secretary, who frequently passed them on to the secretary, John Ellis. In turn, he kept the chairman posted about the trend. Peter Birch, chief executive, was also aware of the trends. The board itself had asked not to be told how the count was developing. As for Deloitte itself, as Peter Jeffrey remembers: "We never tried to hide that we were passing information to Abbey."

Meanwhile, Abbey National held in reserve a plan for a second distribution of proxy forms on March 23 should it then seem necessary to boost a flagging turnout. However, voting got off to such a brisk start that by March 17 this extra mailing, which would have cost approaching £1 million in postage, was abandoned as needless.

As part of its campaign against conversion, AMAF tackled Deloitte on a number of points. In particular, as the ginger group recorded in a press notice of March 28, it requested an assurance that no inkling of the voting trends was being given to anybody at Abbey. Answering this approach, Deloitte told AMAF that information on the subject was being conveyed to the society.

Next, a story in "The Independent" by Patrick Hosking on April 5, quoted Deloitte's Peter Jeffrey as saying: "We are giving [Abbey] an indication of the levels and direction of the vote." Another press report just afterwards conveyed a partly conflicting impression. But from April 5 the belief that Abbey was "home and dry" on the voting took a strong public hold.

When it had become clear that the necessary vote had been secured - a time when the outcome could not be influenced - action was taken to save costs by some cutback in the advertising. John Bayliss, managing director of the mainstream building society business, was asked by Peter Birch, the chief executive, to arrange the cut. Being one of the top people unaware of the voting figures, he queried the move, but Birch, who was in the know, insisted. The reduction probably saved some £200,000.

There was some feeling at the time that Abbey could have been more frank in describing exactly what the reporting position was. But clearly it had taken a policy decision to keep a low-profile stance on the matter at a sensitive stage.

Later on, in its detailed decision on Abbey's conversion, the Building Societies Commission referred to the matter. It accepted the professional independence of the scrutineers and the need for regular reports to Abbey on the volume of proxies received and on progress with the count.

It added: "While the Commission has neither seen nor heard any evidence to suggest that the society made improper use of the reports from Deloitte, there would seem to have been no operational need for the interim reports to cover the direction of voting, as opposed to the totals. It would have avoided unnecessary public misunderstanding and criticism if they had not been given, and that had been said publicly." Abbey maintained that the provision of scrutineers' reports on voting volume and direction was in line with normal practice at most public companies.

Tuesday, April 11, proved cold and wet enough to still fears of an embarrassingly large members' turnout at Wembley. Only 975 braved the weather to attend this key gathering on Abbey National's future. And they were almost outnumbered by the 500 branch staff roped in as stewards and phalanxes of headquarters staff and advisers.

The board assembled up to an hour or more early. Peter Davis, a deputy chairman, remembers passing the time walking from the Arena with Sir Edward Singleton and others in a damp procession under Abbey umbrellas to view the adjacent Stadium the society had also hired.

"It was a great feeling being able to walk through the tunnel and out on to the Wembley pitch," he recalls. Under tumbling rain stewards were posted around the deserted ground where two huge video screens, not destined to be needed, looked down.

Inside the Arena, more accustomed to packed crowds for such draws as the Rolling Stones and Bob Geldof, the audience for Abbey's financial event was contrastingly quiet and sparse. Members took their place, their credentials duly vetted, amid sweeps of vacant plastic seats. Press cameras panned over tracts of unoccupied areas with members scattered widely about. Giant screens, part of the complex relay system, loomed over the hall from different vantage points.

Behind the scenes an array of top talent, including a QC, Timothy Lloyd, Slaughter's Nick Wilson and Tim Clark, and Abbey executives, were gathered with others in the "control centre," the Foxhunter Room. Walkie-talkie gadgetry was to hand for prompting the platform party on any abstruse point. Up front in the hall, the Royal Philharmonic Orchestra was all set to fill adjournments with a programme of light music.

The thinly-peopled meeting convened at 11 am. and, after formalities and an introduction by Sir Campbell, moved on to questions. Speakers' points with microphones were dotted around the hall.

Almost all speeches proved critical of the plan to swap from mutual to company status. While Sir Campbell saw the conversion procedure as an instance of democracy at work, AMAF's chairman, Alex Leaver, found the board's approach, as he remarked after the meeting, "more reminiscent of a Soviet one-party state before perestroika."

Wembley Arena, April 11, 1989. It was a cold day and few people turned up in person for the special general meeting. The landslide "Yes" verdict on the conversion plan was announced here.

One speaker, who said he did not want to put his savings in a bank, warned that a converted Abbey would "be at the mercy of the depraved jungle known as the Stock Exchange where the wolves regularly devour the sheep."

Among detailed contributions was one from a man with closely-argued criticism of the treatment of children's accounts under the conversion procedure, a subject the Commission later focused on. But this member's speech was lengthy and when he remarked he was a solicitor of 50 years' standing, others muttered: "If he doesn't soon sit down, it will be 51 years' standing."

Sir Campbell met complaints from some that he answered

Voted through

many questions himself, as well as chairing the gathering. Eventually, at lunchtime, a motion to proceed to the next stage was approved on a hand-vote, while Alexander Sandison, AMAF's vice chairman, was still waiting to speak. Members then relaxed as the meeting adjourned, the directors withdrew and the vote count was finalised.

Members were next entertained by the orchestra with a medley including Johann Strauss' Blue Danube Waltz, the Radetzky March and the Thunder and Lightning Polka. An unprogrammed incident occurred in one break when fisticuffs threatened as two musicians disputed some professional point. The protagonists were separated by Phil Hallatt as unofficial master of ceremonies.

The formal vote result, when it came at 2 pm, showed that the board had scored a decisive, indeed, overwhelming, success. Of eligible savers, 2.87 million, or 64.6 per cent, voted, 89.5 per cent of them in favour of the change, while 676,000 (64.1 per cent) of eligible borrowers voted, 90.7 per cent of them backing conversion. The turnout of savers was thus more than three times the required 20 per cent. The number of savers opposing the scheme was 300,000 while 62,000 "Against" votes were cast by borrowers.

The figures were announced before the meeting dispersed and were received with a mixture of joy, relief and disappointment.

Sir Campbell Adamson commented: "At last, after many months and a very complicated logistical exercise, our members have made their views convincingly and unequivocally clear. This decision to support our proposal to convert to a public limited company is the clearest indication possible of our members' wishes. I am delighted with the tremendous turnout and the decisive vote in favour."

Looking back months later, Sir Campbell said: "I was absolutely delighted - and not just professionally but personally, since I'd told the Press at the beginning that I'd resign if we didn't get through. Of course, I would have resigned: you can't suggest to your members that you go into a thing of this importance, and remain at the end if you fail. But it made me even more relieved."

In the early afternoon of April 11, champagne was drunk in the Foxhunter Room "control centre" by senior executives and advisers alike.

From Slaughter & May, where four partners and a future partner, Frances Murphy, had worked virtually full-time for a year or more on the project, the most senior, Nick Wilson, later recalled: "Certainly the moment of the greatest elation, so far as we were concerned, was the day of the vote." He returned from Wembley to his City office to find a note reading: "We're all in The Globe" and joined a celebration at that neighbouring pub.

Deloitte now formally reported to Abbey National and the Building Societies Commission on its policing of the vote as scrutineers. It certified that the poll and related procedures had been properly carried out. For the Commission, this was relevant to its coming decision on whether or not to confirm the conversion.

AMAF said it was disappointed at the size of the majority for flotation but not entirely surprised that "the bribe [free shares], unaccompanied by any fair exposition of the arguments against, should have won the day."

As was then to be expected, the pressure group failed with the resolutions it proposed at Abbey's annual meeting on April 26. But it took comfort that the majority then opposed to it was, at just under 3:1 was less overwhelming than the approximate 9:1 which had supported conversion against its own views.

AMAF was also unsuccessful in getting any of its board candidates elected. Instead, members voted back the directors up for re-election, Sir Campbell Adamson, Richard Baglin, John Bayliss, Peter Birch, John Fry, Michael Heap and Jeremy Rowe.

It is recalled that Jeremy Rowe, one of the re-elected directors and a long-standing deputy chairman, had been the sole board member against conversion up to the final decision in March 1988. He had then fallen into step with his colleagues, thereby making the board's choice of the PLC option unanimous, and no hint of the split of view had come to light.

In essence, he would have preferred Abbey National to stay closely linked to housing finance, where he felt it would have ample scope as a mutual, rather than pursue what he saw as the alternative of it becoming a popular bank. This thinking had already led over time to a very real philosophical rift between his view and the commercial, pro-PLC, approach which Peter Birch had brought to the group.

When, around the time of Cliveden, it was apparent that Jeremy Rowe would be an acknowledged unbeliever on a board going all-out for conversion, Sir Campbell raised the issue of whether he wished to resign. This appears to have been brought up as a question rather than a demand. It may be that there were some in the upper reaches of the board who would have preferred the dissentient thinker to quit, while others saw the merit of a solid front in face of opposition from outside.

Jeremy Rowe chose to remain for the time being, but explained to Sir Campbell that provided the membership confirmed the board's decision, he would want in due course to stand down as deputy chairman and retire from the board.

He explained later: "Campbell said: 'Look, Jeremy. It's an honest difference of view. You're out of line with the board.' And would I resign? I said: 'What I would like to do would be to see it through with the board, not rock the boat, and to disappear from the scene if members subsequently ratified the decision.'" Matters were arranged accordingly through a written exchange.

Jeremy Rowe continued as deputy chairman, Peter Davis being appointed as a second holder of that role. Having had a good hearing from his colleagues, Rowe ceased to labour his previous arguments, of course saying nothing of them in public, and played a part as a member of the eight-man board sub-committee on conversion.

"I kept quiet. It goes without saying that I was totally loyal to the board, had absolutely no contact with AMAF, and was involved in the mechanics of preparation. I felt it was very important that the membership should have a choice and hear both sides of the argument," he afterwards recalled.

Apart from his respect for his colleagues' views and his desire to avoid public signs of difference, Jeremy Rowe had a further motive for avoiding the public eye in 1988. Two of his other activities - as chairman both of Peterborough Development Corporation, then due soon to round off its work, and of the Occupational Pensions Board, which was doing a special report to the government - made the prospect of public controversy unwelcome. "It wouldn't have been right for me at the time to become a controversial figure," he remarked. "And besides, I'm not a rebel by instinct."

As it chanced, Jeremy Rowe's Abbey directorship came up for renewal by rotation at the annual meeting in April 1989. Again, had he not stood for re-election, awkward questions would have been raised at a time when the conversion process was far from complete. Therefore, after discussion with Sir Campbell in the winter of 1988-89, he allowed his name to go forward for re-election as a director, and the board routinely re-appointed him a deputy chairman early in 1989. But it was also understood he would step aside later in the year, assuming conversion had by then been accomplished.

Accordingly, he retired on October 30, 1989, after 13 years as a director and 11 as deputy chairman. At that stage he declined opportunities to comment publicly on his departure.

As time has moved on, however, the now chairman of the Family Assurance Society has been prepared to reflect on his position as sole dissenter. An industrialist of long experience, with the formal mien of a City figure, he still cherishes his background in bricks and mortar.

He explains that he favoured the "whole ethos of housing and to some extent social objectives," which he saw as represented by building societies. Also, after seeing his London Brick taken over by Lord Hanson, he feared the effects on quoted companies of bid threats and of "short-termism" pressures for constantly rising profits.

Summing up, he says: "I think it was really the fact that, at the end of the day, Abbey National would become a clearing bank and its distinctive role in housing finance probably be watered down by entry into other activities. I became very convinced that we [Abbey National] could accomplish all our long-term objectives while remaining mutual. Only history will now provide the final verdict but I certainly wish Abbey well in the course they have taken." Jeremy Rowe would be knighted in the 1991 New Years Honours List.

13

"WELL, ER .... YES"

ONCE Abbey National's membership had given its landslide vote for company status, many thought the scheme certain to go ahead. But conversion faced one more big test, the need for its confirmation by the Building Societies Commission.

From the first, the Commission and its chairman, Michael Bridgeman, made it clear that this procedure would be no mere formality with the plan being waved through on the nod.

The Commission arranged a two-day confirmation hearing on May 17-18 to receive oral representations on Abbey's proposals. Previously, just after the April ballot, Abbey had, under prescribed procedures, publicly invited representations on its plan. These came in written form from 215 interested parties, including AMAF, whose detailed arguments against conversion were presented in a 37-page paper, with appendices.

All the written representations were passed to Abbey, which answered them by early May, conveying its responses to the Commission. Fifteen "representers," AMAF among them, wished to make oral statements.

While the Commission was not judging the policy of converting - members had already done that - it was legally obliged to refuse the all-clear in any one of four sets of circumstances. One was if information material to the members' decision had not been made available to all those eligible to vote. Another was if the vote did not represent the views of members eligible to vote.

Further grounds for refusal, also under Section 98 (3) of the Act, would be serious doubt whether the Bank of England would give the new company a banking licence, or breaches of the law or the society's rules.

Since the Bank of England stood ready to give the licence (authorisation), and Deloitte, as scrutineers, had endorsed the correctness of Abbey's vote procedures, attention focused principally on the other tests. In particular, much play was made by AMAF and some others with the argument that Abbey had been insufficiently even-handed in putting the pros and cons of conversion to members.

AMAF had further criticisms as to the supply of information and on other matters, including the denial of the special meeting it had requisitioned and which would have brought its opposition views before members. All these and other opposition points were strenuously rejected by Abbey National.

The Commission's chairman had, back in 1988, stated its view that a converting society's board would be failing in its fiduciary duty if it merely put to members those points supporting its case. Then, in July 1988, in a Commons debate on conversion Regulations, Peter Lilley, MP, then Economic Secretary to the Treasury, spoke rather similarly, saying: "The Regulations and the Commission together provide powerful safeguards against a society tempted to put only partial and one-sided information to members."

It may be wondered why there was such insistence on a fair and balanced presentation of the conversion pros and cons, since the Act does not exactly require this, at least in so many words. The answer seems to lie in the interpretation of a society's wider "fiduciary duty," or general obligation, to its members. In taking the view it did, the Commission had no doubt fortified itself with its own legal advice about what "fiduciary duty" implied.

Before the confirmation hearing Abbey faced a new sort of marathon, the preparation of answers to the 215 "representations." Graeme Johnston, the conversion co-ordinator, recalls the "long, long days" of labour involved in researching each case and drafting the replies. Frances Murphy, the woman member of Slaughter's main team on conversion, and Timothy Lloyd QC, joined the team conducting this work.

Eventually on the final morning an hour was spent in signing all the remaining replies. Frances Murphy remembers accompanying others in a desperate rush to deliver these responses to the Commission by noon on May 9 only to learn that the deadline was, instead, 5 pm. "We'd been working all night to get these answers in," she recalls.

For AMAF, as a small voluntary group with no paid help, the production of its submission was the product of much effort. The paper was chiefly the work of Alexander Sandison, the vice chairman. Its preparation was no light task for a 74-year old man not in perfect health.

Sandison told the hearing: "Only because I am retired and have been able to devote about 12 hours a day to these matters over the past month or so - not quite every day but on that scale - has it been possible for us to make the presentation we have."

AMAF's paper contained many criticisms of the manner in which Abbey National had presented its case and conducted certain procedures. It concluded in this way: "AMAF submits that these representatives contain many examples of 'material information not provided,' and of reasons why the vote represented the views of members on such matters as the receipt of 'free' shares rather than on conversion itself, any one of which could be sufficient grounds for refusal to confirm .... Taking all these matters into consideration, we submit that the grounds for refusal are overwhelming." It then proceeded to suggest that, after the refusal of confirmation which it hoped for "at least a year should elapse before members are again asked to express an opinion."

The criticisms made by AMAF were in turn rebutted in detail in an 88-page reply, with appendices, from Abbey National.

The Commission held its confirmation hearing - a first-ever use of the procedure, like all else in Abbey's conversion - at Church House, Westminster, a frequent venue for Church of England synod meetings. Chairing it, with a mix of formality and informality, Michael Bridgeman sat with three fellow-commissioners, David Hobson, a leading accountant, Geoffrey Sammons, a prominent solicitor, and Herbert Walden, a noted figure from the building society world.

In opening remarks Michael Bridgeman made it clear that the Commission had a duty to seek whatever information it thought necessary to reach its conclusions, even on points not raised at the hearing.

Abbey National chose a leading barrister, well-known in the litigation world, to appear for it on this occasion. He was Samuel Stamler, QC, a colourful, strongly-built figure with the advocate's classic powers of rhetoric, humour - and conciliation. Timothy Lloyd, QC, the building society expert who had long advised Abbey, appeared with Stamler. Both were instructed by Slaughter & May, whose Nick Wilson, Tim Clark and Frances Murphy attended the hearings, as did John Fry with colleagues including Graeme Johnston.

"Well, er .... yes"

Alex Leaver, chairman, Alexander Sandison and Professor Robert Perks spoke for AMAF. A few individual "representers" put their case in person, but the great majority of the submissions were summarised into groups of arguments, almost all objections to conversion. These, along with the related Abbey answers, were read into the record by Commission staff. Points made ranged from a complaint that lending from a bank would be more inflationary than that from a building society to detailed contention about the law's effect.

The two long days of hearings were hot and, like many occasions in the approach to Abbey's conversion, coincided with a train strike. At the close of the first day Michael Bridgeman said they would reassemble next morning - "God and British Rail willing."

Making Abbey's application for conversion, Sam Stamler argued that confirmation ought to follow unless one of the conditions listed in Section 98 (3) applied. However, as to the first of these, he asserted that all material information had been made available in the transfer document, while no other communications contained material misinformation. As to the second condition, confirmation should, he argued, only be refused if the Commission considered that the vote held did not represent what the members wanted. It could not be held that, by not putting AMAF's arguments before the membership, Abbey had withheld material information.

Many other points were covered by Stamler, particularly claims by AMAF, that, in various respects, Abbey's presentation of its case had shown bias and other alleged defects.

For its part, AMAF strongly pressed many of its arguments, while acknowledging that, given more time, certain comments included in its representations would not have been made. Among other arguments, Alex Leaver, the protest group's chairman, suggested that what had taken place was "an election campaign where only one side could reach the main body of the voters."

Addressing the point sometimes made, not by Abbey, that a large enough "pro" vote removed all doubt as to the rightness of confirmation, Alexander Sandison said: "I cannot see how the law can be interpreted to mean that, if the vote for conversion is big enough, it does not matter how unbalanced the presentation of the argument was."

A particular point raised by Alexander Sandison and others concerned the position of children's accounts, where the form of the title, as to whether the child's or parent/guardian's name appeared first, could influence share rights. This was a subject on which more would be heard.

After the hearing Abbey National faced a tense wait for the Commission's decision. The passing days brought it ever nearer the moment when final preparations had to be made for the last prelude to conversion, the big cash-raising share issue scheduled for June 15. The Commission, on its side, was confronted with a major work-load in considering the unprecedented Abbey case.

Nine days after the hearings, on May 27, the Saturday of a bank holiday weekend, John Fry was driving to horse trials with his wife, Diana, and one of his daughters. On the journey he received a call on his car telephone.

It was from the Building Societies Commission chairman, who was working in his London office on Abbey's application, and had a question to raise. But first, he advised the Fry party to park in a layby in the interests of road safety, a cause close to his heart since his wife, June Bridgeman, is in charge of this subject at the Transport Ministry.

The query concerned the designation of children's accounts, and caused John Fry to alert Graeme Johnston, who in turn contacted the systems expert, Brian Leary. A hectic weekend was then spent investigating past and current practice as to the order of child names on accounts. Several days later an extra session of the confirmation hearing was called at the Commission's offices to probe the topic further.

It now appeared that, under a system phased out by 1984, accounts of children operated by an adult (in whatever form they had been opened) had been entered in the computer with the latter's name first. The effect under the conversion scheme was to deprive such children of membership rights, including entitlement to the cash payment.

Full sorting out of this problem would have taken so long as to wreck the flotation programme if this had to be done before confirmation. In the event the Commission decided not to delay but to require Abbey to agree to vary its arrangements (something its legal procedures allowed for) to provide for a review of the 250,000 or so accounts in question.

This was done and the Commission then confirmed the conversion plan, also issuing under the Act a direction that errors in voting rights flowing from the children's accounts situation should be formally disregarded. An assurance was further obtained that Abbey

National had no intention of treating existing borrowers any differently after conversion.

The Commission's decision statement giving its clearance, dated June 5 and handed personally to Abbey representatives, including John Fry, by Michael Bridgeman, the chairman, who himself helped photocopy it, came at the very last moment consistent with the flotation timetable. "Another 24 hours and we would have had to pull the [extra shares] issue," John Fry recalls.

The confirmation, although very welcome, was however coupled with considerable critical comment on the very subject of the presentation of the pros and cons of conversion which had dominated much of the previous controversy. The Commission found that the section of the transfer document headed Advantages and Disadvantages of Conversion was the section "where members could reasonably have expected to find the fair and balanced assessment of the consequences of the proposal, and the board's conclusion based on that proposal, which members were entitled to receive. It did not measure up to that standard."

One point singled out for criticism was what the Commission considered a "failure to bring out the change of objective - the duty of the board to run the successor in the interests of its shareholders, not in the interest of the investors and borrowers as such."

As to Abbey's not having circulated opposition views like those of AMAF, the Commission observed that "if a board chooses perfectly properly not to put the views of others to its members, the duty on it to put a fair assessment itself is thereby the greater."

Summing up, the Commission concluded that: "Part IX (on advantages and disadvantages) falls far short of the balanced assessment of the consequences of conversion which members of a society can reasonably expect from a board. It shows neither the care, the quality of analysis nor the objectivity which the Commission would expect of the board of a major building society and its professional advisers; the significance of that shortcoming is increased by the partiality of the earlier material put to members; there was, as a result, a significant deficiency in the information available to members as a basis for their decision."

At the same time, the Commission was satisfied that the deficiency it saw in the information provided had not, given the scale of members' majority vote for conversion, been material to their decision. The Commission also made clear its view that the selection of the conversion scheme chosen was "a proper decision for the board." Many aspects of the case were reviewed further, with detailed comment, in the 99-page decision which gave the green-light for conversion.

It is understandable that some of the Commission's remarks caused a sense of hurt, even resentment, when they were first read. But, unwelcome as were the critical parts of the decision, the society, recognising that the Commission had a job to do, decided to play the matter coolly. Messages to the Bank of England, the future supervisor, and the government explained why Abbey National did not consider the criticisms justified.

A passage in the directors' report in the 1989 Abbey National report and accounts recorded: "It is worth stating that the Board of Abbey National was surprised by and totally rejects these criticisms. Given the close involvement of the Commission at every stage, and the Board's very careful approach to the whole conversion process and to the Transfer Document specifically, these criticisms were unexpected; not only did the Commission comment upon the numerous drafts of the Transfer Document which were submitted to them, they also made some important contributions to the actual wording of the document."

In its own annual report in July 1989, the Commission commented that Abbey had accepted most of the comments it had itself offered on the non-statutory parts of the Transfer Document. But, the Commission added, Abbey: "chose not to take all of them - including many of those on the part which was later to be the subject of most of the criticism and the confirmation stage."

The Commission also noted the pressures the Abbey timetable had meant for itself. At much the same time it issued new guidance which is likely to mean that the formalities of any further conversion of a building society will take more time than did Abbey National's.

Whether any other future society, aiming to convert, would challenge the Commission's interpretation of the law in relation to the need for a balanced presentation of the case remains to be seen. A senior Abbey National personality said later: "I think it's entirely unreasonable to expect a management to put forward the alternative view when it believes in a certain view. If, say, ICI is seeking to take over company XYZ, they would not in their offer document set out the pros and cons. They would say that the board had decided the acquisition was in the group's interest; they would not go on to survey the downsides and say that, if XYZ doesn't perform, the following would be the consequences."

That there were no lasting hard feelings against the Commission is suggested by a subsequent comment by Abbey's chief executive, Peter Birch: "I have to say, on reflection, that Michael Bridgeman acted impeccably and was very fair throughout. He never took sides, he treated us fairly and equitably and he never said a thing, or wrote anything, that was biased in any way. We may not have liked what he wrote, and indeed we didn't like what he wrote at times, but he had a very difficult job to do."

The Commission later indicated that the reasons for the form and extent of its decision statement were several. Its first objective was to reassure the society and those making representations that their points had been considered.

Another intention was to give societies with similar plans and aims in mind for the future an indication of the position the Commission takes on general points concerning the interpretation of the relevant sections of the Act and of the way in which it considers it should use its discretion under it. Such statements (like policy statements in the Commission's Annual Report) create a presumption that the Commission will follow them in any subsequent case, although it has a duty to hear arguments to the contrary put to it in any case, and to take account of other facts and arguments it considers relevant in the case.

A further important objective of the Commission's decision statement was to provide the Court, in the event of the matter being taken to judicial review, with a sufficient statement of the Commission's findings of fact and law, and the reasons for the exercise of the discretion allowed under the Act, for the Court to apply the appropriate tests.

Finally, the Commission had as one of its purposes to foster the observance of what it saw as "good practice," by both encouragement and criticism.

A serious worry for Abbey and its advisers in early June 1989 was that the Commission's decision was so critical that some people might reason that a refusal of confirmation would have been a more logical conclusion from its argument.

AMAF certainly thought this and said as much in a Press notice on June 6: "There is a point of law here which might be appropriate for judicial review, if anyone can afford it."

Of course if any party were to appeal to the Court for judicial review of the decision by the Commission as an official body, the time taken for the case to be resolved would completely disrupt the flotation timetable.

However, there was no time to brood on this risk and, fingers crossed, the planners forged on with preparations for the looming cash issue.

14

THE FLOAT AND THE QUOTE

THE FINALE of Abbey National's long march to company status was its share-launch on the Stock Exchange in its new PLC form through a giant dual-style flotation. Thus, not only was the worth of the converted society spread among qualifying members through a 100-share free handout as a prelude to the market bow. The same members were also offered the chance to buy further shares on cheap terms via an issue to raise for Abbey the near-£1 billion fresh capital needed for its future banking role.

The idea was that the extra shares should be priced to make them, for those with money to spare, an offer hard to refuse. This share offer was one of the largest ever made by a public company, while the two-part distribution would allot shares to up to five million people, most of them new to the world of Stock Exchange investment.

As soon as the Commission's go-ahead had cleared the way for the issue to proceed, Abbey tackled the delicate task of pricing the extra shares. With the offer due to be unveiled on June 15, to permit final float and conversion on July 12, there was no time to be lost. Just four days on from the Commission's decision, the Abbey directors who had steered the PLC process held a summit with their City advisers in the unlikely setting of the Penta Hotel, Heathrow Airport.

The venue was picked to suit Sir Campbell Adamson, the chairman, and Peter Birch, chief executive, who had just flown in from pre-launch talks with big Scottish institutions. The Heathrow gathering, which took the form of a PLC sub-committee, also included Peter Davis, a deputy chairman and himself a City man, John Fry, the conversion team leader, John Ellis and another executive director,

James Tyrrell. Tyrrell, the finance chief, had prepared key papers for the meeting, as had Kleinwort Benson. the group's merchant bank.

These Abbey top people were joined by Kleinwort's David Clementi, the director skilled in big flotations who had helped shape Abbey's conversion scheme, and by Stuart Stradling, head of corporate finance at Rowe & Pitman, Abbey's main brokers, who was in touch with the pulse of the market.

The party had to reconcile several objectives in putting a price tag on this members-only "rights" issue. As with all such offers, the cost to subscribers should be low enough to afford the sweetener of some instant profit, a "premium", when dealings began.

The price had also to take account of the ratings of such comparable shares as those of the large clearing banks and the TSB. It was necessary, too, to stick to commitment made in the transfer document that the price would be in the 120p-160p range and that not more than one-third of earnings would be paid out as dividends.

Another factor was that, although 1989 was a boom year on the stock market, the banking sector, bedevilled by Third World debt, had been faring worse than the average. Despite its lack of international lending, Abbey National could not expect its own share rating to be uninfluenced by this. Neither could Abbey escape the effects of the languor in the mortgage market, where high interest rates were damping business after the previous year's tax-induced surge.

Although the society's first-half had brought no net profit rise, there were expectations of a 10 per cent increase in profit and dividend for all of 1989. But it was thought unwise to count on a bigger rise than that. All this suggested that a price rather below the 140p mid-point of the 120p-160p span would now be right. At the same time, it would be wrong for the group to be floated at too low a price.

Against this background, the following approach was proposed to the price-setting gathering: The big banks on average were trading at prices yielding prospectively around 7.3 per cent, assuming some dividend uplift for 1989. Abbey National, though a newcomer, looked as appealing as they - perhaps rather more so - with its good track record and unburdened as it was by dud international loans. It could reasonably be expected to settle down to trading on a prospective yield, assuming a one-tenth rise in the 1989 dividend, of 7.25 per cent.

On that assumption, a launch price which could return 7.9

per cent on the notional 1988 dividend, or 8.7 per cent on the likely higher one for 1989, looked right. There would then be room for the shares rapidly to move up to a premium of, say, 20 per cent, after which they would be yielding 7.25 per cent, broadly in line with the market's 7.3 per cent average.

This result would be achieved by a sale tag of 130p. But with an issue of £1 billion at this price, Abbey believed its 1989 dividend might possibly not quite be three times covered by earnings.

The solution to this problem, hit upon by James Tyrrell and Kleinwort, was that the issue should be "tweaked down" to £975 million. On this basis, all the sums fitted the desired framework. The rather lower total (a net £890 million after conversion costs) would still raise enough to meet the Bank of England's requirements and leave some spare capital in hand. Moreover, in the period ahead, Abbey's capital, as reckoned by the Bank in the supervision context, would still continue to build up thanks to retained earnings and the "drip-feed" of amounts released from the PLD.

On this basis, an offer price of 130p a share, to yield a notional historic 7.9 per cent, was decided on. A slightly lower figure was considered but rejected. There was considerable debate whether Abbey's shares ought to be rated, and priced, higher. Peter Birch, in particular, queried whether the assumptions about the market's valuation of Abbey National were not too pessimistic.

It was finally agreed, however, that it would be best not to take too much for granted through an ambitious offer price. Although the advisers expected Abbey's shares to gain ground over time, they thought it preferable to play for safety and avoid any risk of a "flop" by making the shares cheap enough to achieve a sell-out and a good initial premium. After all, whatever the opening price gain, it would be going exclusively to members and not to outsiders. These arguments, in which all the advisers concurred, were decisive with the Abbey bosses.

David Clementi, who has been the issue maestro for such privatisations as British Telecom and Electricity and who had been assisted in work on the Abbey share pricing by his colleague, John Williams, afterwards said of the decision: "There are absolutely no marks for overpricing a rights issue, considering it's going to the people who already own you."

Of the strong rise in Abbey's shares to well over 200p in the months after flotation, he added: "I expected them [Abbey] to be at the top end of the bank range, as they are. Nevertheless, they were the new boys on the block. And my very strong advice was that they would do better, as the new boys at school, to come in modestly - and prove over a period of time that they were the best thing in the banking sector, rather than shout from Day One: 'I'm best.'"

Abbey remained very happy with the pricing decision, which ensured a successful launch. The modest offer figure also proved a safeguard against embarrassment when the shares dipped to near 140p before embarking on a long steady climb. The subsequent strength was further encouraged by the strong showing exhibited by Abbey National's trading results for the whole of 1989.

The group's profits before tax rose by 21 per cent to £501 million while net profits advanced similarly to £323 million. Holders of the 560 million free shares naturally enjoyed the benefits of the shares' good performance, just as did the owners of the 750 million shares sold for cash.

The next stage, within a week, was to be the announcement of the share offer and the price, on June 15, known as "Impact Day." This would set off a 29-day countdown to conversion and the final stock market float on July 12. Just beforehand, there was to be the customary underwriting in which a group of City banks agreed, for a fee, to buy up, at the offer price, any shares not bought by Abbey's members. These underwriting obligations would then, as usual, be sold on to hundreds of City investment funds.

Meanwhile, other preparations for Abbey's double-style share issue were hustled ahead. Charts programmed the jobs falling to Abbey National departments and branches at key points in the crucial months from Impact Day to the shares' float on July 12.

Lloyds Bank now moved centre stage in its role as receiving bank and registrar. Lloyds had been chosen some time before on the strength of its high reputation and prominent position in these fields, and on the basis that it could handle the record volumes of work in question. It was involved in all the relevant planning, and most closely in the timetable from Impact Day through the period while share applications flowed in and up to the despatch of certificates to the new shareholders.

Lloyds' task was a complex one. While Abbey itself would send out the share applications and related documents, Lloyds was responsible for assembling the share register, processing returned applications and getting out the certificates, both for shares due under the free entitlement and for those purchased under the offer. The certificates themselves were, under an innovation agreed with the

Stock Exchange, to be the final documents of title. This avoided the old-style procedure whereby a provisional letter was later swapped for the certificate itself and so simplified matters for everyone.

Refund cheques due to applicants not receiving all the shares applied for, would be sent at the same time. Despatch of the certificates would be spread over two days before the first stock market dealings, the Stock Exchange having allowed this arrangement in view of the huge volume. Normally, the Stock Exchange restricted the mailing to the eve of an issue's final launch in order to prevent the emergence of an informal "grey market." The despatch would be handled by a number of mailing houses.

The membership eligible to receive the distribution of 100 shares came to 5.5 million, a figure further refined and updated compared with the original 5.6 million voters' list. About half a million people figured on the list as both savers and borrowers and so were due for a double-entitlement. It was decided to treat these as two separate members in the planning arrangements. Those receiving both free and extra shares would normally, however, be sent a combined certificate.

Estimating the likely take-up of the extra share offer was a difficult business. Abbey's working assumption, after research, was that, at the very most, four million might apply. Arrangements were made accordingly.

The handling network Lloyds set up to deal with returned applications and later distribution of certificates was in five different regional locations, each containing two receiving bank centres. In view of the record volume expected, Lloyds, while running three of the locations itself, sub-contracted the work in the other two respectively to Bank of Scotland and Midland Bank.

The idea was that each location would handle up to 800,000 applications, one-fifth of the reckoned four million maximum. Similarly the five would also share the task of organising the final issue of the share certificates, taking 1.1 million apiece of the 5.5 million total.

Abbey had its carefully-prepared list of 5.5 million eligible members, as used for the conversion ballot, which was in essence the raw material for compilation of its shareholders list. It had decided, though, that it would be wrong simply to send free shares to every name on the list with no further formality at all. Thus it introduced the so-called "validation" procedure.

Under this, members were first asked, in April-May, through

The float and the quote

the Free Shares Form, to confirm their entitlement and give their full name, with their address and detail of one account. In doing this, people effectively "booked" their free shares and were listed to receive them by the date of conversion and first dealings.

By the time of the share offer in June, three million people had validated in this way. These particulars had then been passed to Lloyds for inclusion in the register it was building of those to receive certificates.

The share application process next gave members two further opportunities to validate. The application form itself contained a space for this purpose on the reverse for those only wishing to collect their free shares and not to subscribe for more. In addition, the fact of applying for extra shares was treated as a validation. Thus, the share offer further boosted the inflow of names to Lloyds in connection with its preparation of the register.

Altogether, just about 4.3 million had validated in time to be sent certificates by the start of share dealing. This total was made up of some 2.7 million desiring only their free shares, and 1.6 million who also bought extra shares.

However, this left as many as 1.2 million who did not do the simple paperwork needed for selling their shares on time. Abbey's response was to send these people in mid-July a "letter of allocation" telling them that 100 free shares were due to them and asking them to validate. Within a few weeks, 500,000 had replied and claimed their shares. Fresh action was later taken to reduce this "core" of members who had not validated; this total went down to some 450,000 after a reminder in November.

Remarkably enough, more than a year after conversion, £90 million of free shares still remain unclaimed.

An implication of these figures is that the number of share certificates needing despatch before conversion was, at 4.3 million, considerably less than the 5.5 million which had once seemed possible.

Within Abbey itself, the extra shares offer meant a wave of fresh work for many and involved another major exercise for Derek Roylance and his purchasing staff over the printing and despatch of 5.5 million application forms, and of copies of the 15-page mini-prospectus which accompanied it, with a pre-paid envelope. This operation culminated in the packing and mailing of these documents over three days after the offer's unveiling. A full 82-page prospectus, chiefly of interest to professionals, was also produced.

The float and the quote

Abbey National's branches stood braced for crowds of members drawing cheques to finance share applications. It was estimated that 90 per cent of the cash for this purpose would come from Abbey savings accounts. The "direct debit facility" to pay by an

Impact Day. Sir Campbell Adamson (left) and Peter Birch stroll from the model house at the Honourable Artillery Company's City ground after revealing the 130p flotation share price tag.

instruction on the form from an Abbey account was designed for customers' convenience and to diminish the inrush to branches.

There was some discontent later where members elected to debit "notice" accounts, without having responded to previous

Green faces and green suits under a green umbrella - an off-beat way of publicising the share float price tag.

reminders to give the required notice, and consequently found the payment attracting an "instant withdrawal" penalty. In some cases, for individual reasons, a debit was not possible.

Applications lodged in branches went by courier to the receiving centres.

Elsewhere in Abbey's organisation, the computer systems, banking and finance departments stood by to handle the huge payment volumes both through debit to Abbey accounts and by cheques on Abbey or the banks. A complex chart sketched the flow of application money by the various methods to Lloyds' collection accounts. It was prepared by Malcolm Holdsworth who, as well as setting up the Abbey National Sharelink dealing arrangement, was closely concerned with planning the payment methods and liaising with the Stock Exchange on the certificates' design.

June 15 was fixed as "Impact Day," the date when, following the clinching of the underwriting, the cash issue would get underway and the price unveiled.

Final clearance for the offer had been given at a board committee of Abbey National PLC the previous day at Kleinwort's offices. The committee, consisting of Sir Campbell Adamson, Peter Davis, Peter Birch, John Fry and James Tyrrell, met along with representatives of Kleinwort and Slaughter & May.

At this important gathering, the committee also gave its seal of approval to the prospectuses, application forms and underwriting agreement, along with other documents concerning the issue. It further approved necessary amendments to the transfer agreement between the society and its successor PLC as well as new articles of association for the PLC. In addition, it gave formal authorisation for Treasury (money market) operations to proceed in the normal way

Lord Rockley, a non-executive director and vice chairman of Kleinwort Benson, Abbey's merchant bank.

Jeremy Rowe, Abbey's deputy chairman. Also chairman of his family company, London Brick, before it was taken over by Lord Hanson, he was an initial dissenter to the decision to cast off mutual status. Having had his say, he decided to close ranks to support his board colleagues in a unanimous vote in favour of conversion.

under the new structure. The full board had already endorsed the June 9 share price decision on June 12.

In line with tradition, Abbey National's mega-issue was sent forth on the world with plentiful razzmatazz.

Going one better in stunt spectaculars has become the hallmark of top-line flotations and the debutante building society's was no exception. While Marines had abseiled Britannia House to reveal the price of the giant BP share sale, and British Airways had traced its own in the sky, Abbey National brought the house down - literally - with its announcement.

A model dwelling, topped with a roof shaped in Abbey's logo, was built on the Honourable Artillery Company's City ground. When journalists had assembled, a puff of smoke tinged with Abbey's red and green corporate colours demolished the outer walls revealing the "130p" in waist-high figures. Then Sir Campbell Adamson and Peter Birch strode, with Buster Keaton-aplomb, from the wreckage to greet the waiting press. A mile away, Kleinwort's skyscraper, which for days had been adorned with the Abbey logo, now sported the "130p" share price tag.

More wackily, green-clad couples, with greened up faces, perambulated under green roof-style umbrellas with "130p" picked out in red. The stunts were the brainchild of John Harben, who worked throughout as public relations adviser on the conversion project.

A separate Press conference was held in Edinburgh with a live TV link to the HAC event. Unfortunately no reporters turned up by the time it, and its London, counterpart, were due to start so the resourceful Charlie Toner, who was presiding, pulled in local branch staff to play the missing journalists' roles. Together they staged a lively question and answer session, which came across the video link to the City as convincingly as the real thing.

The price was well received in the Press, which viewed it as a good buy and predicted a premium of 30p or more when dealings began. There were some favourable comparisons of the new arrival with the currently-depressed clearing banks, but also remarks that Abbey was not launching in a specially cheerful climate. Commentators noted that no full-year profit forecast was given.

The expectation of an instant rise in the price appeared to justify the decision on the offer figure. Public interest in Abbey was heightened by the fact that the free shares, if sold, could bring a £160 gain. A good deal of such profit-taking was expected.

Although the minimum application was set at 100 shares, costing £130, the maximum was put at a hefty 3.75 million shares. The earlier transfer document had foreshadowed a "high" maximum: the effect of the figure named was that wealthy members, charities and the like could put in for big amounts.

Whether such applicants could expect large allocations, and profits, would depend on the overall response, since Abbey promised that every applicant could count on at least a 100-share allotment. Ten days were allowed for receipt of applications from when mailing of the offer documents was complete on June 19 until the closing date of June 29.

Terms of the underwriting had been fixed the previous day, June 14, the agreement being held in escrow (suspense) overnight. The primary underwriters were Kleinwort, S. G. Warburg and three other City banks well-known to Abbey, Baring Brothers, Samuel Montagu and UBS-Phillips & Drew. After John Fry had, on the morning of the 15th, formally confirmed that no sudden catastrophe had occurred, the main underwriters set to work in the usual way on-selling participations to numerous sub-underwriters among the City's investing institutions.

Jim Hamilton remembers that, for his firm's part of this operation, he mobilised and briefed some 60 Kleinwort Benson Securities' salesmen, who then rang a long list of City institutions. The underwriting was successfully concluded in a few hours. The underwriting commitment extended over the 29-days until completion of the float-conversion on July 12: fees are higher when underwriters' exposure exceed 30 days.

The underwriting fee paid by Abbey was 1.32564 per cent of the issue, out of which the brokers received 0.17564 per cent instead of the standard 0.25 per cent and the sub-underwriters one per cent against the usual 1.15 per cent. This concessionary rate, which reflected the operation's big scale and relatively modest risks, followed recent practice for big privatisation issues. (The underwriting was not put out to tender, a kind of auction procedure which had been used in the government's major BP share sale in 1987.)

As John Fry later pointed out, Abbey thus broke the City's usual underwriting cartel for the first time in a non-privatisation issue, excluding the somewhat special TSB case. In the latter instance, the City institutions, being able themselves to subscribe for the issue, had conceded still more favourable underwriting terms. As disclosed in the Prospectus, the underwriting bill to

Abbey amounted to £15.2 million exclusive of VAT.

There was one aspect of Abbey's launch which, in theory at least, involved an element of uncertainty. The road to conversion for the building society had been cleared by the Commission's confirmation, but that consent by a public body was one that could be opposed in an appeal to the Court for judicial review. If such an action were to get under way, conversion would be held up. So the underwriting agreement, in addition to the normal provisos, contained a provision addressed to this risk. The flotation could be called off in the event of an application to the High Court.

This provision was kept very low-key, being alluded to in the prospectus in these words: "The Underwriting Agreement may be terminated, inter alia, in certain circumstances outside the control of the company."

The agreement itself, though not published, was, as the prospectus showed, open to inspection at Slaughter & May's offices. Those concerned touched wood that nobody would take up this opportunity and get ideas about making an appeal.

As it happened, Abbey and its advisers had already had one heart-stopping moment on this aspect on June 13, the day before the underwriting was settled. One Andre John-Salakov then applied to the Court for an order to forbid the operation of the Commission's confirmation of Abbey's conversion. But this request was turned down by Mr Justice Otton on the grounds that the applicant, who was not himself an Abbey member although his children and ex-wife were, lacked the legal standing to pursue the matter.

Nicholas Wilson remembers hurrying to the Court that day after a report that the case was coming up had been spotted in the Communist "Morning Star" newspaper. He also found Alexander Sandison of AMAF, which was itself still considering taking the matter to judicial review, although with little hope of doing so given the potential expense. This was confirmed on June 27 when AMAF announced that it would not proceed to take action for judicial review of the confirmation.

AMAF said that it had leading Counsel's advice that "the Building Societies Commission had misdirected itself on a point of law" in confirming the conversion, that permission for judicial review "would almost certainly be granted" and that the review "would stand a very good chance of success." However, it had not the resources to face the possibility of having to meet the Commission's costs should it fail. It had asked the Commission to waive any costs that might become due to it, were the case brought. But, scarcely surprisingly, the Commission refused to support such a move against itself.

This statement assuaged much of the remaining worry that conversion might still be stopped in its tracks by a legal move. After this, matters progressed smoothly towards the climax of flotation and conversion taking effect simultaneously on July 12.

The extra share offer proved a sell-out, with 1.6 million people putting in for two million shares, 2.7 times the 750 million up for sale.

On Saturday, July 1, Abbey's chiefs got together with their advisers in the Glass Room at Abbey House to settle how to allocate the over-subscribed issue.

Sir Campbell was presiding and the party included Peter Birch, John Fry, James Tyrrell, Graeme Johnston and Phil Hallatt, along with Lloyds Bank's Bill Paine, Kleinwort's John Williams and Slaughter's Chris Saunders.

Decisions were a little complicated by the fact that another rail strike had delayed posts in the previous few days. To cater for this, Abbey had agreed to receive applications which arrived late, so long as they were posted by the cut-off date, June 28. Since it was not known on July 1 how many might still be held up, the basis of allotment had to leave some shares in hand for late arrivals.

The Abbey chiefs decided once more to adopt a very democratic basis, recognising the equal rights of all members.

Thus, applicants for up to 600 shares received all they asked for, while everybody seeking more got a 775-share allotment. (800 was the next quantity above 600 which could be applied for).

The method of apportionment has been described as Abbey National's "last great mutual decision" in catering for the fact that all applicant members had equal votes by giving them a more or less equal allotment. A more sharply scaled allocation, geared to the size of applications, was rejected for the same reason. This was a blow to wealthier savers who had put in for large amounts of shares, hoping that big allocations would yield them bonanza profits. At least a few applicants had wanted to buy millions of shares.

A more difficult question had been whether to set the maximum permitted purchase at 800 or 775. The former round figure might well have been chosen but for the need to keep some shares in hand against late applications.

Peter Davis, the deputy chairman who had been at the pricing session and the key board sub-committee meeting to give the issue plans their last finishing touch, participated, at some remove, in the allocation gathering. A keen trout fisherman, he was booked to spend that Saturday on the River Test. He proposed that he should keep to his plan but to take a mobile telephone, enabling him to keep touch with Abbey House.

After fishing for some time, he called up John Fry who explained that the decision had followed a basis known in advance to the deputy chairman, who duly added his assent.

The over-subscription strengthened hopes that the shares would show an immediate profit from the start of dealings. Lloyds Bank prepared to despatch all the share certificates (for both free and bought shares) over the two days, July 10-11, with the aim that all members should receive theirs by July 12.

On that date, Vesting Day, the transfer agreement would be fulfilled and the long-planned changes would all happen together. Conversion would thus take effect, the cash issue would go "unconditional," and Abbey National PLC would be in business with its shares launched on the Stock Exchange.

Oversubscribed. It is June 1989 and John Ellis (left) and Peter Birch, with Lloyds Bank staff, hold some of the 1.6 million share applications.

Slaughter & May's Tim Clark planned the completion of the complex formalities, culminating in the synchronisation on Vesting Day of the Bank of England's authorisation of Abbey National PLC and the listing of the latter's shares on the Exchange.

Six days earlier, on July 6, Abbey's executive chiefs held a staff rally at Wembley for some 800 managers from round the country to mark the approaching big date. Part of its aim was to assure staff that, after its change to PLC status, Abbey National would still be the same friendly group as before.

John Bayliss, head of the mainstream building society business, said that after conversion Abbey National would be a retailer of personal financial services and, as such, would be neither a building society nor a conventional bank. It would position itself as an approachable and highly professional provider of professional services to the personal customer, with an improving branch network and developing range.

"Conversion for us is just the starting line," he added. James Tyrrell and Charlie Toner also put colleagues further in the picture about the way ahead.

After the over-subscription.
Another cartoonist's view of the successful flotation.

" I GOT THE IDEA FROM THE ABBEY NATIONAL SHARE OFFER— ITS CALLED SCALING DOWN "

One theme of the get-together was "natural selection," the concept, popularised by Charles Darwin, of species' ability to adapt successfully to change. Peter Birch wound up his concluding speech by saying: "Natural selection made Abbey National the best among building societies. Natural selection has made us the first to convert to public company status. We have everything to ensure that, in retail financial services, Abbey National is the natural selection."

On July 12, a milestone day in Abbey National's annals, the long-prepared switch to company status went through right on time. After the split-second process for the bank licensing and share-listing, the new PLC slid down the launch chute in a perfect float. History was made as this first-ever building society to go commercial took its place among Britain's five largest stock-market traded bank groups.

After the Vote, the Float and the Quote had been achieved

The new stock market recruit continued to log up records.

The float and the quote

After Abbey's flotation, its shares were the most actively traded of any on the Stock Exchange in the July-September 1989 quarter. The average deal (and special arrangements allowed for small sales to be bundled up) worked out at £13,600 as the investing institutions moved in to pick up Abbey shares. Demand from City funds was stimulated because Abbey, on July 17, became one of the top hundred stocks in the FT-Stock Exchange ("Footsie") index, which some big investors like to mirror in their own holdings.

The competitively priced Abbey National Sharelink dealing service came into operation with the launch. After a quiet first two days, it handled its largest-ever turnover, 50,000 share transactions, on July 14. The fact that its volume fell short of the highest previous estimates reflects the fact that the total Abbey share sales also did so. It was reckoned that Abbey National Sharelink handled three-fifths of all business in Abbey shares through the four and a half months of its existence.

As the Stock Exchange later noted, selling of Abbey's shares was not as brisk as many had expected. It is true that by the end of 1989, institutional investors had amassed 24 per cent of the shares, a percentage which later rose to more than 30 per cent. But loyalty led the great majority of former members to retain some, if not all, their shares. In mid-November 1990, 16 months after conversion, 3.8 million former members still had some share stake in the converted society. At that time, the institutional investments (those of over 5,000 shares) accounted for 37.6 per cent of Abbey National's shares and the millions of smaller shareholdings for 62.4 per cent.

On July 19 Sir Campbell Adamson hosted a dinner at the Savoy to mark the successful conclusion of the conversion-flotation project. The guests were more than 30 Abbey staff and advisers who had played key parts in the marathon, with their partners. Speeches by Sir Campbell and Kleinwort's Lord Rockley recalled incidents along the way, including Nick Wilson's solution of a daunting legal problem with the help of whisky and a bath.

Other festivities followed in the country two days later. But already there were ominous signs that all was not well over the distribution of share certificates.

15

THE THUNDERCLAP

THE EMERGENCE of the disaster in which half a million Abbey National share certificates went missing - amid a series of other upsets - may be likened to a thunderstorm. Distant rumblings, not too alarming, first made their presence felt. Then the sound grew louder and the storm, punctuated by sharper cracks, rolled closer as the atmosphere darkened. Tremors continued, with the watchers apprehensive of the unusual turbulence. Then a dazzling lightning flash illumined the scene followed by a shattering thunderclap. This, in its turn, was succeeded by brighter skies as the tempest passed, leaving in its wake much wreckage to be cleared up.

The first signs that something was wrong came on July 12, the very day Stock Exchange trading started. Phil Hallatt, a deputy secretary and skipper of the logistical plans, remembers it well.

"We started to receive large volumes of phone calls in the information office from people complaining that they hadn't received their share certificates and so were unable to deal. We assumed, at that stage, that the delay was due to difficulties in posting the huge numbers of certificates." Abbey spoke repeatedly to Lloyds, whom Abbey had contracted to act as receiving bankers, pressing that any hold-ups should be sorted out in discussion with the Post Office.

Next day, July 13, John Fry, the director who had led the conversion team, was telephoned by Lloyds. "They said they were frightfully sorry they hadn't been able to issue some share certificates," the result, it seemed, of late applications. These were now to be sent on.

Within a day there was another message that Lloyds had discovered three tapes (lists) of people who had not been sent their free shares. "I said: 'you'd better get those out as soon as possible.'"

At the same time newspapers were carrying reports of angry shareholders protesting at the non-arrival of their certificates. Words such as "botch-up" were now being used in references to Abbey's big exercise in popular capitalism. There were widespread stories, too, of refund cheques not being received. Those who had put in for big blocks of shares, and so were due for large repayments, were specially incensed at the delays in getting their money returned. There was also evidence of documents arriving with garbled addresses.

At first the Abbey chiefs hoped the delayed arrivals reflected understandable hold-ups in the ambitious operation to get record millions of certificates out by the share-launch day. Checks by Lloyds and the Post Office had not shown up any pronounced hitches.

John Fry remembers leaving for the weekend of July 15-16 knowing there was a problem but not yet feeling unduly concerned. It was realistic to think that, if 4.3 million certificates were posted on Monday and Tuesday, the last of them might not arrive by Friday. Probably, by Saturday, the great bulk would have been delivered.

He recalls thinking: "After all, nobody has ever before attempted to get definitive share certificates to everybody within a week of the first day of dealings. And Lloyds were telling me they had sent out the vast proportion of the 4.3 million due to go." He felt, and said to the chairman over the weekend, that there was some need for people to show patience. Two weekend Press commentators took much the same line.

Of the first fews days when Lloyds and the Post Office strove to reconcile the numbers handed over by individual mailing houses and received by the Post Office, Phil Hallatt says: "We were unable to believe other than that there was a postal problem. And, in the absence of any information from Lloyds, except that they believed the Post Office had not, for some reason, delivered a certain number of shares, we were having to put to our shareholders information which was at best vague. At that particular time we had no idea of the size of the problem."

However, as the days went on, the symptoms of trouble grew more ominous and it was soon clear that something far more grave than at first suspected was involved. Phil Hallatt remembers: "The worrying thing was that, whatever the differences between Lloyds and the Post Office, they could not explain the large volume of calls we were getting. They were arguing over relatively small numbers, whereas we were receiving so many phone calls that we believed the problem was much larger.

"The situation became so bad it was impossible to get an outside line from here in Abbey House to phone anywhere. We were reduced to using mobile phones to contact Lloyds, who were under equal pressure on their switchboard. We were receiving thousands and thousands of calls."

John Fry takes up the story at the point just three business days after the first share dealings. "Things got worse on Monday and Tuesday, July 17 and 18. Our switchboard was jammed and we were hearing that switchboards of newspapers and the BBC were also jammed by callers."

Faced with the seemingly inexplicable disruption, John Fry summoned representatives of the registrars and postal services in order to bring home the scale of the emergency and to search out its cause.

"On Wednesday the 19th, I sent for Lloyds and the Post Office. I said to them: 'Something is terribly wrong. Lloyds is telling me they've delivered all the certificates to the Post Office, every single one of them. And you, the Post Office, are saying you've delivered them all. This cannot be, because we're still inundated, we're getting branches under siege, telephone switchboards under siege.'"

Steps were immediately taken to accelerate the process of reconciliation between Lloyds' figures for despatches, and the Post Office's for receipts, of documents. These were to reveal that Lloyds' arrangements could not readily identify the trail from register database to printing firm and thence to mailing house and the Post Office.

From then on senior people at Lloyds sent Abbey daily reports on the situation and regular high-level meetings were held. Over the week from July 24 advertisements were published apologising for the problems and advising non-recipients to complete a reply coupon and return it to Lloyds. For a time the heart of the problem still proved elusive.

The state of siege reached, for a while, what must have been unparalleled dimensions for any corporate accident, its sheer scale being due to the huge numbers later revealed to have been affected when the chief trouble was finally traced.

Phil Hallatt recalls that Abbey had 150 operators at British Telecom - probably the largest such team in use in any flotation - answering telephone queries on its behalf and using set scripts provided. But neither these, nor the staff of Abbey's own Information Office, could cope with the peak flood of calls still coming in.

Meanwhile, newspapers were closely tracking the development of the certificates saga, themselves often besieged by calls from disgruntled shareholders. The events were now gaining new labels such as "fiasco." The Stock Exchange, too, showed concern at reports that some free shares had, in error, been issued twice.

John Fry, who until the last few days had successfully achieved each objective on the long road to conversion, now felt the shock of the unlooked-for calamity.

On the occasion of the celebratory Savoy dinner on July 19 he recollects: "For the first time, I felt that day totally exhausted, utterly and completely deflated. I'd never known a crisis of such proportions which one didn't know the answer to."

Tackled by the Press as to what had gone wrong, he was forced to take the line: "I'm asking Lloyds, whom I've contracted to do this job, to tell me what the hell has gone wrong, and I cannot get an answer."

Abbey was critical of Lloyds' control systems which were not measuring up to the quality of controls it had itself used in its own earlier mailings, and which could track the successive movements of each batch of documents.

The crisis endured for some days more as the tide of complaint and enquiry about missing or mis-directed certificates, and refunds, swept through branches and swamped the telephone system.

"We had branch staff being spat at, some actually physically assaulted. Telephonists had to be sent home in tears and I had several people on the phone who were incredibly rude," John Fry recollects. He was also dismayed, when taking part in a radio phone-in programme, to speak to two people, one of them unemployed, who had borrowed five-figure sums to apply for shares and were still awaiting repayments.

Eventually the explanation of by far the worst element in a multi-part problem came to light.

On Friday, July 28, an anonymous letter was received at Abbey House. Addressed to the Shares Department, headed "To whom it may concern" and signed "an anonymous friend," it stated that Abbey National share certificates were being burned at a property at Greenwich in south-east London. It mentioned a company called Business Mailing Services, which was one of the mailing houses used to despatch the certificates.

Phil Hallatt recalls the moment of the crucial clue's appearance. John Fry was in his office discussing questions on the very subject of the certificates when one of his staff signalled insistently through the glass door.

The two men looked at the letter, then took it to John Ellis, Abbey National's secretary. Momentary doubts whether the letter might be a hoax were quickly put aside. Lloyds were immediately told, as were the police, who visited the site the same day. As John Fry said later: "Then the whole debacle unfolded."

Next morning there were Press reports that the police had discovered the charred remains of large numbers of Abbey National share certificates in skips at Business Mailing Services (BMS) in Greenwich.

It was a real-life scene to rival the plots of any of Sir Arthur Conan-Doyle's detective novels.

BMS was one of five mailing houses used by Lloyds to despatch Abbey certificates. Although one of the smaller houses employed, it appears to have been allocated one of the largest, if not the largest, individual proportion of the total certificates. Arrangements with it were made via Midland Bank, to which Lloyds sub-contracted some of its task, while retaining overall responsibility.

Shocked as the Abbey chiefs were by the discovery of the burned certificates, they now felt better placed to grapple with the problem. In close consultation with Lloyds, it set in train swift remedial action. The regular, high-level Abbey/Lloyds meetings already instituted controlled this process.

As a first step, Lloyds closely vetted its records in the direction where trouble was suspected. By noting all the certificates where refund cheques had been cashed or shares traded, it identified certain gaps where there were no signs of such activity. This process mapped out areas of non-activity and so presumed non-receipt of certificates and repayments.

The findings were strong circumstantial evidence that in the areas in question certificates had not in fact been sent out. The gaps identified became known as "black holes."

Such "black holes" were discovered in almost all the batches of documents conveyed to BMS for despatch. Geographical areas containing notable "black holes" included Essex, Lincolnshire, Norfolk, Suffolk, Yorkshire and parts of Scotland.

To beat the problem quickly, the certificates due in each "black hole" were reprinted and at once despatched to the shareholders without a specific request for replacement being awaited. As a precaution against any possible duplication, measures were taken against use of the originals.

As for recipients around the fringe of "black holes," replacement certificates were prepared and held ready to be issued upon application. The same procedure was followed with refund cheques due in "black hole" areas.

So rapid was this process that by August 15, 450,000 replacement certificates had been issued, the majority against requests by letter or newspaper coupon or through Abbey branches.

Altogether, it is estimated that up to 530,000 certificates had gone missing from the original issue. As this is around one-eighth of the entire 4.3 million, it is scarcely surprising the losses caused such turmoil.

The rubbish skips in south London where charred remains of numerous Abbey National share certificates were discovered.

The distribution of certificates was also bedevilled by other problems of lesser size, all needing rapid sorting out. For instance, some 135,000 addresses were garbled and checking was needed that the mail in question had arrived. More than 100,000 free share certificates went out two days late, while over 17,000 sets of free shares were mistakenly issued twice and had to be reclaimed.

At this hectic time matters were further complicated by many members who were not eligible for shares, or who had not "validated," believing that they were also victims of the upset.

In the drive to correct the errors, various measures were taken. Replacement claim forms were provided in branches and through newspaper advertisements to assist claimants, while many shareholders were written to individually. It was arranged that delayed refund cheques could be credited to an Abbey account, backdated to July 12.

On August 4 Lloyds published a second advertisement apologising to Abbey National and its shareholders for what had gone wrong and including a further reply coupon.

Thus, gradually, the storm subsided and with little over a month from first share trading the rapid fire-fighting operation had put right most of the mishaps, though final clearing up took longer. Nor did the damage to the previously successful image of the flotation, or the blow to those most involved, fade quickly.

Abbey saw the heart of the problem as the shortcomings in Lloyds' control over certain procedural aspects of the share issue and in the selection of one particular mailing house. Behind this, it believes there lay an under-estimation of the work involved in the unprecedented operation.

John Fry makes the point that Abbey National was particularly exposed by what happened. "There had been no other issue where every single shareholder was also a customer and, in addition, was perfectly free to walk away and take their business elsewhere."

As to the whole affair, he felt "incredibly angry, particularly so because one couldn't persuade the Press to see the matter in its true light. When everybody looks back on it, they'll still talk about the 'flotation fiasco.' What they actually mean is the registrar-share certificates fiasco."

Phil Hallatt adds: "We had planned what we believed was an absolutely first-class product [the new-style definitive certificate]. And then we were faced with a problem of an immense size where we did not have access to the source material to answer the queries coming to us. It was a nightmare."

In due course a director of BMS was charged with criminal offences, including plotting to burn Abbey National share certificates, while five other people faced related charges. At the moment of writing the case is still before the courts.

Abbey National afterwards sought compensation from Lloyds for what had gone awry. The negotiations were handled by John Fry and John Ellis. A settlement was reached, which has been widely reported to be worth some £15 million, a figure there is no reason to doubt.

At Abbey National PLC's annual meeting on April 10, 1990, Sir Campbell Adamson described the settlement as "an extremely good one" but declined to state its amount. He added that the figure agreed on had been rather higher than it would otherwise have been because it was not being divulged.

He also told the assembled shareholders: "Nothing will get over the inconvenience to the members who didn't get their certificates or their refunds and nothing can really pay us back for the loss of image we've had from so many people."

At the height of the lost certificates calamity. The cartoonist's pen is wounding.

"I'm in for the long term — I hope to receive my shares by then"

Formally summing up the essentials of the unfortunate episode, Sir Campbell also explained: "Following a competitive tendering process, Lloyds Bank, who I believe are the market leaders in this field, having been involved in many privatisation issues, was successful. A number of problems did occur, the most serious of which involved destruction of certificates at one particular mailing house and this is a matter which is now the subject of criminal charges. I should like to offer my sincere apologies to all those shareholders who were affected by the problems and the inevitable delays in dealing with the large volume of enquiries which resulted."

While the share certificates drama was mounting, one day was lightened by a pleasant interlude for which, however, some of those invited could scarcely spare time from the more urgent crisis at hand.

Planned well beforehand, the occasion was a day of festivities laid on by the groups which had acted as advisers in the conversion marathon, including lawyers, merchant bankers and public relations people. It was a "thank-you" to the main personalities and their supporting staffs who had taken part in the prolonged task. The party, arranged by John Harben, the public relations consultant, was held on Friday, July 21, at Stocks, the Hertfordshire country house which once served as the Playboy Club's country arm.

Among various entertainments, including archery and mud-biking, which followed lunch, the high spot was a cricket match between an Abbey National team, skippered by John Fry, and an advisers' eleven, captained by Slaughter's Tim Clark. Noted cricket stars joined in on each side, Imran Khan playing for Abbey and Dennis Lillee for its opponents.

After the work, the team at play. Stocks, July 21, 1989, the scene of Abbey National's victory team at the celebratory cricket match. The team are: (standing, left to right) Graham Baker, Malcolm Holdsworth, Stuart Dyble, Derek Blackburn, John Godley, Peter Birch, (sitting, left to right) Steve Montague, Norman Wilkes, John Fry, Imran Khan and Trevor Field. Imran Khan was an invited celebrity.

The losing advisers' team. The team are (standing, left to right) Adrian King, Stephen Thomas, Chris Saunders, Peter Jeffrey, Gavin Simonds, John Harben, Paul Thompson, Tim Wise, Tim Clark, Dennis Lillee and David Freud. Dennis Lillee was the opposition's luminary.

The Abbey National team, which included Peter Birch, won, which the advisers did not grudge given the hard road they had travelled together. "We thought it appropriate," remembers Tim Clark, who adds: "I shall now be able to tell my grandchildren that I captained Dennis Lillee."

The thunderclap

On the advisers' side, Deloittes's Peter Jeffrey has the happy recollection of getting Imran Khan out through a catch off Dennis Lillee's bowling. Another player was David Freud, of Warburgs, which had donated a silver cup. This was presented to John Fry, as captain of Abbey National's team, by Sir Campbell Adamson, who flew in by

Mark Boleat, director-general of the Building Societies Association, whose view of the conversion is: "Abbey has an unnerving record of taking unpopular decisions which prove to be right."

helicopter at 6 pm to perform this ceremony.

Unfortunately, given the share certificate crisis, the day was not a relaxed one. John Fry remembers only reaching Stocks two and a half hours late, at 1.30 pm, and twice being called off the field to

A view of the imposing Bank of England in London. It's banking licence was vital for Abbey's conversion and float.

© The Bank of England

take telephone calls on the matter. Phil Hallatt, for similar reasons, never made it at all to play for his side. "Even so, they won without me. I was so surprised," he jokes.

Many further arrangements, and much tidying up of

problems and enquiries, still lay ahead before everything to do with the conversion programme was at last completed.

In November, the legally-prescribed cash distribution to those not qualified to vote, and therefore without share entitlements, took place. These were savers with less than £100 in their accounts on December 31, 1988, or who were under 18 on the vote date of April 11, 1989 and who held investments in the society continuously until the changeover date, Vesting Day, on July 12, 1989.

The payment amounted to 5.83 per cent of the qualifying balance and totalled £5.1 million altogether. It was thinly spread over 3.8 million accounts, many of them very small, and worked out at an average of £1.34 per member. Even so, the distribution gave rise to queries and added to the work of disentangling residual problems.

"After-care" work to clear up disputes following the unprecedented conversion was, not surprisingly, considerable given the many millions of share and cash distributions involved.

A priority task was to sort out the children's accounts with which the Building Society Commission's direction and the related change in Abbey's transfer agreement were concerned. The cases were essentially those where an account had been opened in a child's name for operation by an adult.

As the Commission had pointed out, a number of such accounts had, up to 1984, been entered in the computer records, which formed the basis for the allocation of conversion benefits, with the adult's name first. This type of designation made the adult the member and consequently deprived the child of his or her entitlement to a cash payment. A total of 274,988 accounts were examined following the Commission's ruling.

Account holders were written to and Abbey stood ready to make the appropriate adjustments to its records for each account which was found to have been recorded in a manner contrary to the investor's wishes.

The upshot was that computer records were adjusted, and cash distributions accordingly made, in 99,089 cases. These actions were recorded in Abbey National PLC's 1989 report and accounts, along with an auditors' report by Coopers & Lybrand Deloitte.

Given the detailed rules of the conversion scheme and the possibilities of error in the "de-duplicating" process, it was inevitable that a number of people should have felt they had not received their rights. To deal with cases not solved through the information office and via a "help line" which was set up, Abbey established a complaints procedure which operated - and still operates - under the supervision of Ian Treacy, a deputy secretary of the group. It is run by Ian Hart, a manager in the secretariat, with a staff of 15.

The pattern of complaints reflected the course of events, rising from a mere seven in March 1989 when the detailed scheme was unveiled to 285 in August after the share certificate scandal, and 677 in October. There was then a gradual decline to 521 in December and less than 400 in April 1990. A fresh boost to the numbers came from November 1989 onwards and was caused by disputes arising from the cash distribution made in that month.

In the 16 months to July 1990, when the complaints department was still busy, some 5,500 cases had come before it. Of these, a number arose from a misreading of the scheme by members wrongly thinking they were entitled to benefits from which they had been excluded.

Ian Treacy says that the main category of other complaints concerns children's accounts, but of a different kind from the ones spotlighted by the Commission.

What is in question is where branch staff are alleged not to have carried out customers' instructions precisely in the designation of accounts. Sometimes, an unwished for change of title has been made where savings have been switched to a higher-yielding account. Each case is settled on its merits, with a cash distribution being made where it is thought justified.

Another significant class of complaints has arisen because two people with similar initials in a household were identified in error as one. Here, appropriate cash compensation is paid for the non-receipt of shares since, for legal reasons, a retrospective amendment of the share register and consequent issue of shares is barred.

The compensation has gone up in steps, broadly mirroring the rise in Abbey's shares: by the early summer of 1990, when the shares topped 200p, £210 cash was being offered in lieu of 100 shares.

Ian Treacy is impressed by the dedication some members show in pursuing what they see as a right to the tiniest disputed sum. "The British bulldog spirit of tenacity really comes out. There are a number of people who, if they see a principle at stake where just £4 is involved, will write 20 letters, as well as making £150 of phone calls, faxes and telexes. And then they may threaten us with The Sun and Esther Rantzen."

Ian Hart remembers that, after his name was mentioned on

the Jimmy Young radio programme, the word went round that he could cure any problem. Arriving home late after a day's slog, a complainant might ring his doorbell within five minutes. "I even had a telephone call from a man who had a complaint about Barclays Bank."

Among the millions of communications sent out, there were a few that were in the nature of thoroughly embarrassing mishaps. One computer error, which arose early in 1989, recorded as dead a lady who was very much alive. She received a "We're very sorry to hear..." letter, followed by a stream of mail addressed to her executor.

At first her protests that she was in the land of the living failed to staunch the flow. After Ian Hart had taken the case in hand and sent friendly apologies, with a goodwill cheque for £50, the member responded in the same style: "I am, of course, delighted that I shall be getting free shares, should the conversion go ahead. All this talk of resurrection and conversion is turning me into a religious freak. I am also, of course, delighted with the cheque for £50, which I intend to spend on riotous living."

Another conciliating letter from Abbey was written to a member whose case had been mentioned on the Jimmy Young show. This included a postscript begging that no further publicity should be given to the case and jocularly adding that, because of the flood of correspondence, the writer was getting home so late, his wife thought he must be having an affair. The lady member entered into the spirit of the exchange and in her answer promised no more publicity, adding: "I prefer to be your correspondent, not your co-respondent."

Tidying-up operations continued.

On the financial side, Abbey National found that the shares it had created (1.31 billion) represented a slight over-estimate of what would be needed under the scheme. The number had originally been fixed to allow for all possible requirements. Clarification of entitlements in doubtful cases then showed some surplus to requirements.

Consequently, in September 1989, 29 million shares were sold through a placing with institutional investors. The price was 141p, just below the then market price of 144p and, of course, above the 130p offer price. A further placing later went through at a higher price. At the end of 1989, the old Abbey National Building Society was wound up.

One matter of considerable interest is how far savings were

withdrawn from Abbey National as a result of conversion. AMAF had predicted a considerable outflow by savers disliking the switch from building society status.

Some £450 million, less than expected, was drawn out of accounts to finance the purchase of Abbey National shares. In addition there was some further outflow, but the group has not given the figure, not can it be inferred from published data.

The company's 1989 annual report says on this subject: "Some money also flowed out from the accounts of people who disagreed on principle with our plan to convert. They were a small minority and we are sorry that they chose to leave us."

Abbey National's conversion had one piquant consequence in the context of official arrangements for tracking the levels of money supply in Britain. The transfer of the society into a fresh category - banking - led to the final demise of "M3," the monetary measure that in the early 1980s had been a standard of totem importance, though its significance had later declined.

In its Quarterly Bulletin of August 1989, the Bank of England dedicated a two-page article to the statistical consequences of Abbey National's conversion to PLC status. The opening paragraph said: "The Abbey National Building Society became a public limited company on 12 July, 1989, and was authorised under the Banking Act 1987 from that date. As such it is classified as a bank, rather than as a building society, within the national accounts. This change of classification has far-reaching consequences for the compilation and presentation of financial statistics, and has led the Bank to review the principal monetary statistics. As a result, a number of changes will be made, and others are under consideration. In particular, publication of the broad monetary aggregate M3 will cease."

Abbey National's shares moved steadily ahead after a hesitant performance in the first weeks after flotation, which was perhaps related to the share certificates disaster. Within a matter of months, however, Abbey's stock market valuation had comfortably overtaken that of Midland Bank to make the former building society Britain's fourth largest bank in terms of capitalisation.

In October 1990, Abbey's market worth went above £3 billion and, though subsequently fluctuating, continued around that level, being £2.95 billion at the end of November. This compares with £1.54 billion for Midland Bank, £2.1 billion for TSB and £3.51 billion for Lloyds Bank at the same time. Abbey National's good track record and its lack of problem-vexed international and commercial lending had given Abbey shares a 3.4 per cent yield, the most flattering rating in the UK banking sector, and a 9.1 ratio of price-to-earnings.

By way of recognition for the exceptional efforts devoted to the conversion work, Abbey distributed lump sums of up to a few thousand pounds as a special thank-you to the staff most closely involved in the operation when it was all over.

Everyone had come a long way on the Abbey road.

16

RETROSPECT AND PROSPECT

WHAT characterised Abbey National's conversion and flotation marathon was a great sense of drive and determination to stay the course undeterred by obstacles. Above all, the effort passed the most crucial test of all by being successful.

Considering that, two years before, conversion was scarcely a gleam in the eye for most of the building society movement, the prompt fulfilment of this ground-breaking enterprise must rank as a notable achievement. The boldness which led Abbey National to seize the chance to convert reflected the group's long-established taste for the new.

Of the many features which stand out in this unique and onerous corporate undertaking was its conclusion without the disruption of normal activities. Acknowledging this, Sir Campbell Adamson, the chairman, told shareholders at the annual meeting in April 1990: "My particular thanks go to Peter Birch and his executive team for tenaciously putting through the conversion project while never losing sight of the main priority, the continuing health and prosperity of the business."

An interesting independent appraisal comes from a leading specialist in the housing finance field, Mark Boleat, director general of the Building Societies Association (BSA) and of the Council of Mortgage Lenders.

He believes that the decision to convert from a building society to a PLC was as much a philosophical decision as a business decision, with a presumption in favour of conversion probably coming to the fore even while the Building Societies Act 1986 was going through Parliament.

"In the early part of 1987, when one suspects much of the analysis on conversion was undertaken by Abbey National, there were strong grounds for converting from a building society to a PLC. Societies were suffering severe competition in the retail savings market. In the mortgage market, lending institutions funded on the wholesale markets were taking good business from the societies, which were not easily able to respond because of the 20 per cent limit on their wholesale funding. Another constraint on societies was their inability to increase their capital quickly to fund diversification."

"However in 1988," he adds, "the societies' powers were considerably widened through government action. Those working on the conversion must have viewed these developments with mixed feelings. On the one hand they gave greater flexibility for the building society, but on the other hand they would make it more difficult to justify conversion. Other building societies looked long and hard at the conversion option and the other four of the five largest eventually announced that they had no immediate plans to convert.

"Perhaps the principal policy ground for conversion is that it would allow flexibility, particularly in respect of developments that could not, at the time, be adequately foreseen. This naturally made it necessary to present the plan persuasively to the electorate."

Commenting on the scheme which was selected, he says: "The single key factor in the conversion process was the decision to issue, to all members qualified to vote, free shares likely to be worth about £150. This option was certainly not envisaged when the Bill was drafted; it was only possible because the relevant sections of the Act were so badly drafted. The decision by the Abbey to equate voting rights with free shares was a masterpiece. It meant that no-one would be able to vote who would not qualify for free shares, and therefore there was no large disgruntled section of the electorate."

Noting that time will be needed to show whether conversion has been a success, Boleat pays this tribute: "The Abbey has an unnerving record for taking decisions which are unpopular at the time, but which prove to be right."

Of particular aspects of the conversion saga, perhaps the main feature was the very demanding and pressured schedule, what one participant called "the tyranny of the timetable."

The need for speed derived from the timing of the share float in mid-1989 because of the necessity to schedule Abbey National's large cash call well before the Water and Electricity privatisations.

The pressures of the very strict timetable were felt not only over the completion of large-scale logistical, drafting and numerous other tasks but also in anxious phases like the consultation with the Building Societies Commission on the transfer document, crisis days such as those of the Court case in January 1989 and in the prelude to the Commission's confirmation in June 1989. At such times as these it was felt that the whole project could be put at risk if a decision by an outside authority was not reached promptly.

A non-executive director makes the point that the "breathlessness of it all cannot be entirely dissociated from the banana skins." The implication of this comment is that the controversy over such matters as the exclusion of joint account-holders from share benefits and, perhaps, the share certificates debacle, might have been avoided had there been more time to plan. Whether this is so is of course debatable.

Another issue is the 10-month interval between the immediate announcement of the board's intention to recommend conversion and the disclosure of the outline of the scheme along with the timetable for conversion in January 1989. During this time, as preparations moved ahead and the scheme was being designed, the continuing flow of Press and public enquiries was difficult to answer fully, the more so because of legal constraints and the fact that it took many months to formulate plans fully. Given that the board felt it should take members into its confidence immediately about the

The London International Stock Exchange in Threadneedle Street, whose listing pressed the release for Abbey's share launch.

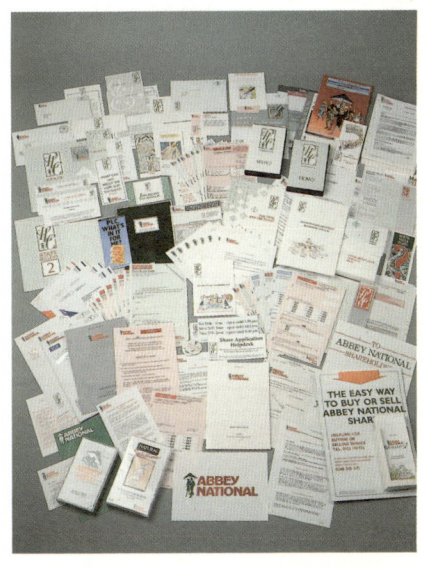

Paperwork in millions. A pastiche of the conversion/flotation documents which required hundreds of tons of paper.

original decision, rather than waiting for some months until preparations were further advanced, it is hard to see how this problem could have been avoided.

Another interesting aspect of the exercise arose from the fact that Abbey needed to be closely guided through the novel process of conversion by specialist legal, merchant bank, accountancy and other advisers. This meant something of a jolt to a society with long-established ways of resolving problems and its own in-house specialist cadres.

The presence in the office daily, over a prolonged period, of so many outside advisers was, as John Ellis, Abbey's secretary, puts its "an experience we had never had before."

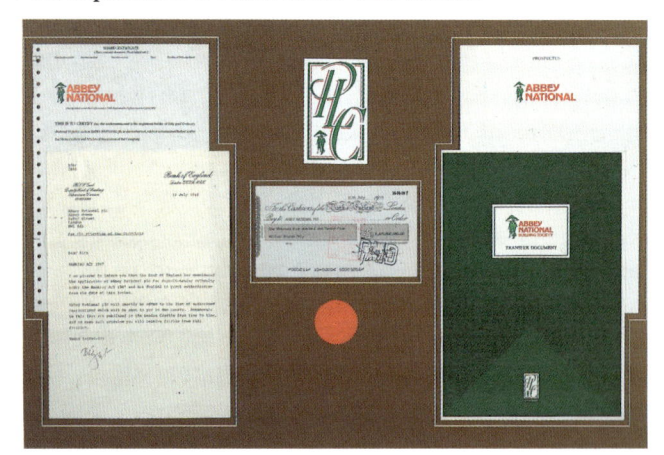

Crucial documents. A new-style Abbey share certificate behind the bank of England's letter signed by Brian Gent, deputy head of banking supervision, giving Abbey National its banking licence.

There seem to have been occasional tensions as a result. But, with hindsight, Ellis stresses the need to be reconciled to a degree of invasion. "I think one of the things we found is that you virtually have to put yourselves in the hands of all these people if you ever attempt anything as big as this. And if I were giving advice to another building society, I would say: 'You have to face up to this at the beginning - that you are going to be involved in trusting a lot of outside advisers to a greater extent than you ever have been used to doing before. You have to put yourself largely in their hands.'"

Abbey's conversion was also an interesting test case of building society members' attitudes as voters. The high turnout and big majority verdict in the ballot for the scheme confirmed members' keenness to back the board's proposals, albeit with a little personal incentive in the shape of free shares. It also showed that attachment to the concept of mutuality represented by a building society's status was more fragile than many had expected.

One of the main conversion tasks - shaping the mechanism for the changeover - was complicated by the obscurity of the Act's conversion provisions even though, as Mark Boleat suggests, the wording gave Abbey conveniently wide scope in creating the scheme.

The Act's conversion sections, seemingly based partly on American practice and partly on procedures followed in the TSB share launch, have been widely criticised. One merchant banker called them "an abomination." The fact that a "friendly" Court case was needed to test and confirm the Abbey scheme's legality is itself evidence of how hard the law was to interpret.

Just how difficult this was as regards on some parts of the Act's conversion sections is illustrated by glimpses of the Court proceedings themselves. At one point, on the subject of Section 100 (8), confining preferential rights to subscribe for shares to savers of two years' standing, the following dialogue took place in Court:

Richard Sykes, QC (for Abbey National): "Of course, your Lordship and ourselves are stuck with the wording of the Act."

The Vice-Chancellor (Sir Nicholas Browne-Wilkinson): "You are stuck with it and I am trying to make sense of it."

Richard Sykes: "It is extraordinary, perhaps, that Parliament did not look more carefully at the wording at the time that legislation was produced."

It was in introducing his judgment in relation to this particular sub-section that Sir Nicholas used the words: "Doing the best I can with this very obscure statutory provision ...."

In the event, Abbey was able effectively to side-step section 100 (8) by not giving its members preferential rights to subscribe compared with other applicants, since no non-members had any subscription rights at all.

One implication of Abbey National's experience of wrestling with the Act's provisions is that any other society converting in future will probably either have to adopt Abbey's model or test the legality of a different scheme in a Court action. Such a society could also, quite legally, make different choices in detail, such as conferring share benefits on joint account holders and possibly relating benefits to the size of a member's savings. If it did, this would be at the cost of a less close tie than in Abbey National's case between voting rights and share entitlements.

Another society could also adopt a scheme radically

different from Abbey's. It could, for example, (like TSB) give no free shares and proceed through an issue of shares by sale only.

The case for some amendment of the Act's conversion provisions, if only to make it less obscure, looks strong. Recently, the Halifax Building Society's chief executive, Jim Birrell, said that any revision of the Act should include redrafting of the conversion sections. Indeed, he and other building society personalities have also talked of a need for much wider revisions of the Act.

Was the effort, and the cost of £66 million, worth it? Has conversion proved the success Abbey National hoped? After all, the group, still predominantly a provider of mortgage finance, has not changed radically in the nature of its business operations since its transformation to bank status.

The answer must be that it is much too soon to appraise the consequences of the new status since Abbey National always believed its strategies in its new form would take time to unfold.

Were it, in due course, to take over a major insurance group or a personal finance concern outside Europe, this would transform the balance of its business in a way not open to a building society. Yet this would still be in line with the corporate policy of concentrating on personal financial services.

If such an acquisition were made against an issue of more shares, it would be an instance of just the sort of development often mentioned in the formulation of the conversion strategy. Some particular benefits, such as the greater range of market instruments which Abbey's Treasury side has been able to use, have been quickly felt, as have the advantages of planning and developing business in a freer legal framework and a less restricted regulatory environment.

More broadly, Abbey National now feels better placed to respond in its own way to opportunities for developing the increasingly broad all-under-one-roof personal financial service it reckons itself well fitted to provide. Clearly, with an existing seven million-plus customer list, and a good image, the group regards itself as strongly placed to compete across a wider field.

John Bayliss, managing director of Abbey's mainstream retail operations and one of the group's top men, explains how he sees the change-over: "I think there is no doubt that the conversion move was right. Looking some years ahead, I do not believe that building societies as such can survive: the competitive pressures on them get harder every day. Yet consider the demand there is for a service that is really comprehensive.

"Take the position of a young person starting work. He opens an account with whoever can attract him and that institution can provide all his financial needs for the rest of his life, insurance, anything you like. That is why we launched a current account, which is the pivotal account where you catch somebody when he first starts work and hopefully keep him, providing for all his personal financial needs for the rest of his life. We want to be in a position to supply just the services to do that.

"In addition, conversion has already allowed us to do things we couldn't have done before, particularly on the Treasury side."

As far as the regulatory side is concerned, he also says: "We don't now have to go down to the Commission and say 'Please may we do this?' We now decide what we want to do, having due regard to the rules of the Bank of England. Our destiny is in our hands now."

Of course, it is not so easy for a mortgage-oriented business like Abbey National's to diversify swiftly in a meaningful way. Nor are fresh ventures often quickly profitable. The new estate agency chain, for example, lost £16 million before tax in the difficult conditions of 1989.

While the selection of major new strategies could take time, Abbey does have the advantage of the continuing "drip feed" into its capital as more reserves are released with the decline of the "priority liquidation distribution." With Abbey well supplied with capital in equity form, known in Bank of England parlance as of the "Tier 1" kind, it has plentiful scope to raise further "Tier 2" capital in "subordinated" loan form, as required.

If capital availability is no constraint on major new moves by takeover or partnerships, prudence itself is likely to dictate a cautious, long-considered approach. Extensive diversification which he witnessed in his time at Gillette, and which did not always pay off, will have made Peter Birch, the chief executive, exceptionally wary about ventures of this kind.

Teasingly, he says: "We've been very careful in the evaluation of other organisations and looking at potential partners. I think we've probably now evaluated every quoted company in the financial services world and the banking world and the City. We've learned a great deal from it and we're wiser as a result."

Even if no bid plans at all are on the stocks, the mere

thought of such scrutiny by the large Abbey National, with its buoyant share price and considerable capital war-chest, is enough to send a shiver through the financial sector.

Abbey National's conversion move and the considerations which prompted it are already proving the catalyst, or at least the forerunner, of much fundamental rethinking on the status of building societies.

It is now widely asserted among the societies that the broadened operating framework created by the 1986 Act is still too constricting. This is the more so since the continuing trend towards a deregulated and competitive environment for the financial industry will be extended afresh by the creation of the European Community's single market after 1992. It was just such considerations as these which helped prompt Abbey National to convert.

Mark Boleat, director general of the BSA, admits that the inflexibility of the legislation causes uncertainty which can be costly not only in terms of money but also of lost business opportunities. Restrictions on Treasury business, the inability to do business in Europe save through a subsidiary and the £10,000 limit on unsecured loans are among examples of current restrictions on building society business which are being found increasingly hampering.

Boleat also points out that societies are finding it necessary to undertake much consultation with their lawyers as to whether or not a particular activity would be permissible under the Act and the associated subordinate legislation.

The need for a new flexibility which so much influenced Abbey towards shedding its building society status has also been underlined by the Halifax's Jim Birrell, who describes the Act as "a frustration. It results in a strong legal input to many decisions. Major reforms will be required by the mid-1990s if societies like the Halifax are not to be forced to take the conversion decision."

Such remarks again afford vindication for the reasoning which led Abbey to switch status.

The Halifax however seems less persuaded by its close rival's belief that conversion offers important fresh access to capital. Birrell notes: "We sympathised with [Abbey National's] argument but in practical terms we still do not see shortage of capital as a constraint. Nothing that the Abbey has so far done or plans to do indicates any need for extra capital. And of course share capital is costly. It has to be paid for in dividends to shareholders whereas societies' reserves are 'free.'"

Thinking among the societies now seems to be swinging towards the idea of a new legal and regulatory framework which would allow societies wider operating powers without a loss of their mutual status. Thus, societies would become "mutual banks" regulated by the Bank of England but still without shareholders.

This could in principle prove a way forward, at least for some larger societies, providing members were content, at a time when the reshaping of the financial sector in tune with current needs and conditions is a continuous process.

A major purpose of the change would be to obtain the broader operating scope for which there is an increasing desire among the top societies. With competition as strong as ever in the financial services world, institutions like building societies with a limited span of functions are increasingly conscious of the handicaps of their legal status vis-a-vis other groups in the market.

Yet the idea of "mutual banks" opens up very wide issues. Such entities would be a novel form of organisation, legally perhaps more akin to the former savings banks now merged commercially within the TSB quoted company than to any other structure. Yet something much more advanced and sophisticated than the old-style savings bank is envisaged in discussions now under way. The introduction of such an unfamiliar category as "mutual banks" evolving from building societies would require very careful thought.

New ways for societies to gain access to fresh capital without a switch to PLC status are also being explored. The Building Societies Commission has outlined plans for a type of "permanent interest bearing shares" which would be sold to investors and could be traded. Such instruments appear, however, more akin to the subordinated "perpetual" floating rate notes issued by banks in recent years than to the true equity shares which only companies can create.

One question raised by the suggestions that building societies might evolve into "mutual banks" is whether such groups' members would be quite satisfied with such a transition. Having seen the (albeit individually modest) share entitlements allotted by Abbey National on its changeover to bank/PLC status, would they not demand similar gains for themselves? Might there not be "AMAF in reverse" campaigns by ginger groups of members urging boards to convert for the sake of share benefits?

It is sometimes argued that, by contrast with the former position in the US, there is no sign of such pressure in Britain. Yet already, bonuses are often paid to members of the acquired society in amalgamations, while the possibility of takeovers of UK societies by foreign banks willing to pay well, to the benefit of members, has lately been canvassed and is not excluded by present law. Any large takeovers of this kind could well stimulate the interest of societies' members in the possibilities of conversion to "unlock," or release, to them the "equity" in their group.

At the same time, operation as a PLC in competition with a mutual is a demanding business since a company must pay dividends on its shares, while a society's reserves require no such servicing. Abbey reckoned that it was efficient enough to be able to shoulder this obligation for the sake of the extra access to capital and the greater operational freedom it acquired. How many societies would be equal to operating in this exacting situation after conversion remains to be seen.

It is certain that no such new entities as "mutual banks" could be created without major new legislation, the mere introduction of which would raise fundamental questions about the governance and control of such institutions, as well as about the future position of smaller building societies.

There is also the question whether it would be quite fair to have "level playing field" conditions operationally between "mutual banks" and a group like Abbey National which had shouldered the trouble and expense of becoming a PLC with a share capital to service in order to gain a freer status. Against this, it could be argued that Abbey's switch to PLC form had been a completely voluntary choice made with its eyes open.

Meanwhile, Abbey National has served as the successful pioneer of conversion, the pathfinder clearing the way through problems and exposing difficulties. Others which may follow will gain from its experience.

How Abbey exploits its new status and develops its unique role as a big bank specialising in personal financial services will only be fully seen over time.

What is certain is that in going PLC, it again - true to its traditions - took the lead and is thus securely placed to reap the gains available to the first society to convert.

It has liberated itself ahead of the pack from a confining operating framework which others are now finding constricting. It has positioned itself to tap the equity capital necessary to finance a big expansion move when such action looks right. In short, it has successfully managed its transition to the commercial sector, where it has full freedom to mould its future course as it desires. And finally, it is most unlikely that Abbey National has lost its well-known capacity to surprise its competitors.

INDEX

Abbey Road Building Society 11, 101
Adamson, Sir Campbell 2, 5, 17, 18, 19, 20, 22, 31, 32, 36, 44, 45, 47, 53, 54, 55, 56, 57, 58, 59, 60, 62, 72, 82, 89, 91,92, 96, 98, 99, 101, 104, 105, 107.108, 109 110, 121, 131, 132, 133, 134, 147, 154, 155, 158, 161, 169, 170, 172, 179
Adamson, Mimi 58
Ageros, Jane 89
Albert E Sharp 86
Abbey Members Against Flotation (AMAF) 9, 12, 89, 93, 95, 96, 97, 99, 100, 101, 102, 103, 104, 106, 107, 109, 110, 129, 131, 132, 133, 134, 137, 138, 139, 140, 142, 144, 157, 176, 188
Argos 34
Baglin, Richard 2, 38, 101, 133
Bank of England 3, 4, 5, 27, 62, 63, 68, 113, 115, 116, 117, 137, 138, 143, 149, 159, 176, 185, 187
Bank of Scotland 151
Barclays Bank 20, 175
Barclayshare 86
Baring Brothers 156
Barnes, John 34
Barnes, Jean 34
Barnes, Kenneth 34
Bayliss, John 2, 18, 32, 33, 37, 46, 47, 81, 89, 101, 129, 133, 160, 184
Bayliss, Maureen 58
Bazlinton, Christopher 101
BBC 17, 165
Bellman, Sir Harold 17
Big Bang 22, 23, 48, 52
Birch, Peter 2, 3, 31, 32, 33, 35, 36, 37, 38, 39, 41, 43, 44, 46, 47, 49, 51, 57, 61, 62, 82, 98, 99, 101, 105, 107, 114, 121, 122, 129, 133, 144, 147, 149, 154, 155, 158, 160, 171, 179, 185
Birch, Gillian 34
Birrell, Jim 184, 186
Boleat, Mark 25, 179, 180, 183, 186
Bond 127
Borer, Ros 5
Bourke, Lorna 101
Bow Group 16
Box, Stephen 73

BP 155, 156
Bridgeman, Michael 9, 69, 70, 71, 137, 139, 140, 142, 144
Bridgeman, June 141
British Airways 155
British Rail 140
British Telecom 3, 46, 86, 88, 149, 165
Broad Street Associates 89
Brooks, Ian 73, 121
Browne-Wilkinson, Sir Nicholas 8, 71, 183
Building Societies Association 12, 14, 25, 28, 30, 59, 69, 179, 186
Building Societies Commission 4, 8, 9, 29, 62, 69, 82, 90, 96, 97, 100, 102, 130, 133, 137, 141, 157, 173, 181, 187
Business Mailing Services 166, 167
Cambridge University 18, 38
Cameron Markby Hewitt 127
Capper Granger 126
Carmichael, Sir John 18
Carter, Douglas 73
Chivers, David 95, 99
Church of England 139
Citizens Federal Savings and Loan Association 15
Citizens Savings and Loan Association 15
Clark, Tim 3, 5, 63, 64, 73, 75, 81, 89, 99, 131, 139, 159, 171,
Clark, Clive 101
Clementi, David 3, 4, 46, 63, 148, 149
Cleveland, Alan 127
Cliveden House 52, 53, 55, 56, 57, 58, 133
Cobden, Richard 11
Collins, John 95
Confederation of British Industry 17, 19
Conservative Party 20, 26, 47
Coopers & Lybrand Deloitte 82, 173
Council of Mortgage Lenders 179
County NatWest 2
Croydon Transport Users' Association 103
Daily Mirror Newspapers 22
Davis, Peter 2, 21, 31, 47, 52, 54 58, 60, 82, 130, 134, 147, 154, 158

Davis, Vanessa 58
Deloitte Haskins & Sells 3, 4, 5, 61, 73, 82, 114, 115, 121, 126, 127, 128, 129, 130, 133, 138, 172
Dunstan, Alan 126
Ellis, John 2, 38, 39, 46, 48, 54, 66, 81, 82, 98, 106, 129, 147, 167, 169, 182
EMI 38
Evening Standard 68
Family Assurance Society 135
Fisher, Peter 88
Foster, Roy 3, 115
Freud, David 121, 172
Fry, John 1, 2, 4, 5, 7, 32, 37, 38, 39, 41, 42, 46, 47, 61, 63, 65, 70, 71, 72, 82, 85, 86, 90, 101, 106, 111, 120, 133, 139, 141, 142, 147, 154, 156, 158, 159, 163, 164, 165, 166, 167, 169, 171, 172
Fry, Diana 58, 141
Garlick, Sir John 20, 47, 52, 82
GEC 20, 47
Geldof, Bob 130
Gillette (UK) 31, 32, 33
Goddard Kay Rogers 31
Gowans, Stewart 3, 81, 89, 90, 101, 126
Granger, Robert 126
Guardian, The 95
Halifax Building Society 25, 51, 55, 58, 184, 186
Hallatt, Phil 73, 82, 125, 127, 129, 132, 158, 163, 164, 165, 169, 172
Hamburger, Otto 95
Hamilton, Jim 119, 121, 156
Hanson, Lord 47, 135
Harben, John 89, 155, 170
Harley, Ian 73, 114, 115
Harris Queensway 21
Hart, Ian 174, 175
Heap, Michael 48, 102, 133
Heseltine, Michael, MP 20
Hill, Lord 12, 17, 18
Hilton, Sir Derek 18
Hobson, David 139
Holdsworth, Malcolm 86, 87, 154
Hosking, Patrick 129
Hoskyns 34
Hull University 127
Humphreys, Sir Myles 21, 47
ICI 143
Imperial Group 18
Independent Broadcasting Authority 17
Independent, The 101, 129

Jeffrey, Peter 3, 114, 127, 129, 172
Jenkins, Dame Jennifer 21 47, 54
Jenkins, Lord 21
John Kitching Associates 41
John-Salakov, Andre 157
Johnston, Graeme 3, 73, 81, 90, 138, 139, 141, 158
Jones, David 86
Khan, Imran 171, 172
Kilbane, Sandra 84, 85
Kleinwort Benson 2, 3, 5, 6, 46, 61, 62, 63, 73, 81, 88, 89, 90, 119, 123, 148, 149, 154, 155, 156, 158, 161
Kleinwort Benson Securities 3, 119, 121, 156
Knighton, Bob 81
Labour Party 26, 29, 56
Laing & Cruickshank 40
Law Society 21
Lawson, Nigel, MP 27, 59
Lazards 53
Leary, Brian 81, 83, 141
Leaver, Alex 95, 98, 99, 101, 102, 131, 140
Lewis, Andrew 95
Lillee, Dennis 171, 172
Lilley, Peter, MP 59, 100, 101, 138
Lines, Thomas 101, 109
Lloyd, Timothy 46, 67, 82, 131, 138, 139
Lloyds Bank 3, 5, 52, 88, 123, 150, 151, 152, 154, 158, 159, 163, 164, 165, 166, 167, 169, 170, 176
London Brick Company 17, 47, 135
London Life 128
Mabey, Simon 16
Mailcom 126, 127
Management Centre Europe 36
Marshall, Sir Arthur 37
Marshalls of Cambridge 37
Mathews, Terry 70
Maxwell, Robert 22
Midland Bank 151, 167, 176, 177
Mirror Group 22
Morning Star 157
Morrison, Sara 20, 47, 48, 52, 53
Morton, Sir Stanley 17
Murphy, Terence 36, 38
Murphy Miller Ginsburg 36
Murphy, Frances 73, 132, 138, 139
National Economic Development Council 19
National Farmers Union 17
National Opinion Poll 125
National Savings Committee 19

National Society 11
National Trust 47, 52, 54
National Westminster Bank 3
Nationwide Anglia Building Society 51
Nelson, Tom 70, 71
Nestle 33
Netherthorpe, Lord 17
Newsnight 60
Occupational Pensions Board 47, 134
Otton, Mr Justice 157
Oxfam 101
Paine, Bill 88, 158
Perks, Professor Robert 101, 109, 140
Peterborough Development Corporation 17, 47, 134
Post Office 7, 84, 85, 164, 165
Rantzen, Esther 175
Rees, Hugh 18, 47
Registry of Friendly Societies 29, 69
Riley, Hazel 111
Robinson, Simon 82
Rockley, Lord 3, 161
N. M. Rothschild 55
Rowe, Jeremy 17, 18, 47, 52, 56, 58, 59, 60, 82, 102, 133, 134
Rowe & Pitman 3, 119, 121, 148
Royal Philharmonic Orchestra 131
Roylance, Derek 84, 85, 152
Runcie, Dr Robert 38
Rybczynski, Professor Tadeusz 53, 55
Sainsburys 21
Sammons, Geoffrey 139
Samuel Montagu 156
Sandison, Alexander 95, 96, 98, 99, 100, 101, 103, 104, 106, 107, 110, 132, 139, 140, 157
Saunders, Chris 89, 90, 158
Scottish Widows 109
Securities and Investments Board 90, 91
Sharelink 86, 154, 161
Singleton, Sir Edward 20, 47, 130
Slaughter & May 3, 5, 6, 61, 63, 64, 70, 71, 73, 75, 81, 82, 88, 89, 90, 99, 127, 131, 132, 138, 139, 154, 157, 158, 159, 171
Smith, Chris, MP 100
Spalding, John 25
Stamler, Samuel 139, 140
Stamp, Lord 12, 101
Stamp, Elizabeth 12, 101
Standard Life 109

Stent, Sue 126
Stewart, Ian, MP 26, 27, 29, 30
Stock Exchange 1, 3, 4, 5, 7, 22, 62, 68, 72, 73, 85, 87, 88, 118, 121, 131, 147, 151, 154, 159, 161, 163, 166
Stradling, Stuart 120, 121, 148
Sturge Holdings 21, 47
Sun, The 175
Supple, Professor Barry 101
Sykes, Richard 183
Tarmac 18
Tennant, Sir Iain 21, 47, 52, 53, 82
Thatcher, Margaret, MP 13, 128
Thomas, Stephen 114
Thornton, Clive 18, 20, 21, 22, 23
Tillett, Paul 16
Timberlake, Tim 17, 18
Toner, Charlie 38, 122, 155, 160
Treacy, Ian 66, 174
Trustee Savings Banks 7, 29, 46, 63, 64, 67, 110, 117, 118, 148, 156, 177, 183, 184, 187
Tyce, John 40
Tyrrell, James 2, 21, 38, 46, 81, 114, 115, 117, 122, 148, 149, 154, 158, 160
UBS-Phillips & Drew 156
Villiers, Charles 2
Walden, Herbert 139
Warburg Securities 121
S. G. Warburg 3, 119, 156, 172
Watts, Lesley 63
Welsh Development Agency 47
Wilkes, Norman 66
Williams, John 5, 63, 73, 81, 89, 149, 158
Wilson, Nicholas 3, 6, 63, 64, 70, 71, 73, 99, 131, 132, 139, 157, 161
Wise, Tim 73, 89
Woolwich Building Society 51
Wycherley, Sir Bruce 17
Young, Jimmy 175